D0457622

The Quotable Birder

The Quotable Birder

EDITED BY
BILL ADLER JR.

THE LYONS PRESS

Printed in the United States of America

Designed by Compset, Inc.

10 9 8 7 6 5 4 3 2 1

Library of Congress Cataloging-in-Publication Data is available on file.

To Stephanie Faul,
who got me interested in birds in the first place

Contents

Acknowledgments

What can I say? Without the help of Jessica Smith and Tracy Quinn, *The Quotable Birder* would never have been possible.

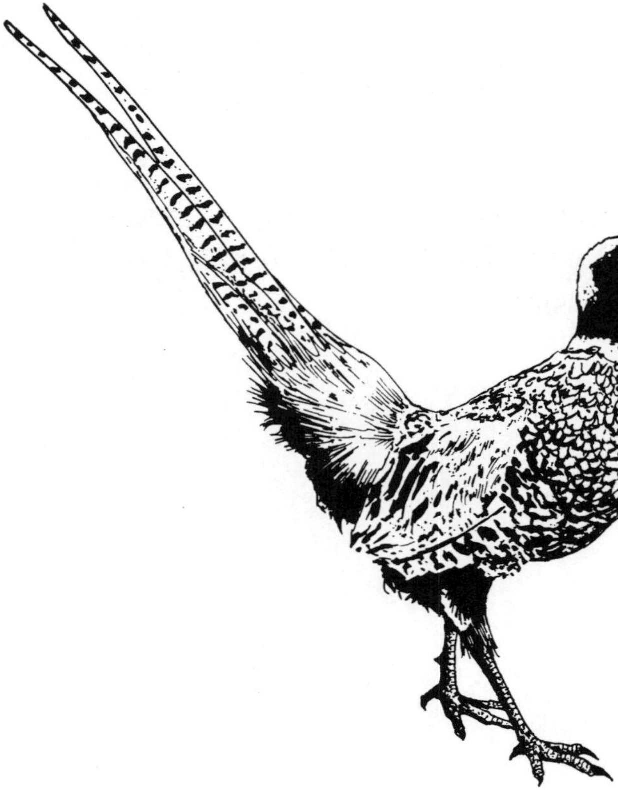

Introduction

People enjoy listening to their music and are in awe of their flight. But more than anything we love to write and talk about the wonder of birds. The fascination with birds goes beyond birdwatchers and nature-lovers. From poets and politicians to actors and athletes, no one can resist referring to our feathered friends to help explain the human experience (or make fun of it), or simply to comment on their grace and beauty.

The Quotable Birder isn't just about birdfeeding, bird watching, and individual species of birds. People frequently mention birds when talking and writing about love, war, fate, life, history, health, and, of course, Thanksgiving dinner. People adore all kinds of birds—from parakeets to puffins. As a society, we have pet birds, we go on bird watches, we feed birds. *The Quotable Birder* takes an interesting look at what we say about birds and how birds color our everyday speech. *The Quotable Birder* also takes a look at how frequently birds have appeared in literature throughout time as well as oral traditions such as proverbs and nursery rhymes. Quotations about birds are a part of our history, culture, and literature. You'll find that people from all walks of life have had something to say about birds, ranging from the serious and somber to the comic and complimentary.

By reading *The Quotable Birder,* you'll not only learn a lot about birds, but you'll be amused and entertained; you will also uncover insights into our society and culture, and, perhaps, yourself.

—BILL ADLER JR.
WWW.ADLERBOOKS.COM

Flying, Soaring, and Aviation

Words are inadequate to describe the flight, the many variations in the formations, the alternate beating of wings and sailing, the beauty of the flocks in silhouettes against the white mountain and the blue sky, and the exhilarating poetry of it all in this primeval wilderness country.

—ADOLPH MURIE, ON THE MIGRATION OF THE
SANDHILL CRANES, FROM *A NATURALIST IN ALASKA*,
"CRANES AND CARIBOU"

The reason birds can fly and we can't is simply that they have perfect faith, for faith is necessary to have wings.

—JAMES M. BARRIE, *THE LITTLE WHITE BIRD*

———◆·◆·◆———

"Inventive man" has invented nothing—nothing "from scratch." If he has produced a machine that in motion overcomes the law of gravity, he learned the essentials from the observation of birds.

—DOROTHY THOMPSON, *THE COURAGE TO BE HAPPY*

Can you imagine any better example of divine creative accomplishment than the consummate flying machine that is a bird? The skeleton, very flexible and strong, is also largely pneumatic—especially in the bigger birds. The beak, skull, feet, and all the other bones of a 25-pound pelican have been found to weigh but 23 ounces.

—GUY MURCHIE JR., "SONG OF THE SKY"

Volumes have been written concerning observations on the flight of birds. The marvel has been why do soaring birds maintain themselves in space without flapping their wings. In fact, it is a much more remarkable thing to contemplate why birds which depend on flapping wings can fly.

—J. S. ZERBE, "THEORIES AND FACTS ABOUT FLYING," *AEROPLANES*

King Henry: But what a point, my lord, your falcon made, And what a pitch she flew above the rest! To see how God in all his creatures works! Yea, man and birds are fain of climbing high.

Suffolk: No marvel, an it like your majesty, My lord protector's hawks do tower so well; They know their master loves to be aloft, And bears his thoughts above his falcon's pitch.

Gloucester: My lord, 'tis but a base ignoble mind That mounts no higher than a bird can soar.

—WILLIAM SHAKESPEARE, *KING HENRY VI*

Speed, bonnie boat, like a bird on the wing,
"Onward," the sailors cry;
Carry the lad that's born to be king,
Over the sea to Skye.

—SIR HAROLD EDWIN BOULTON, "SKYE BOAT SONG"

The great bird will take its first flight . . . filling the world with amazement and all records with its fame, and it will bring eternal glory to the nest where it was born.

—LEONARDO DA VINCI, "THE CODEX ON THE FLIGHT OF THE BIRDS"

But flies an eagle flight, bold and forth on, Leaving
no tract behind.

—WILLIAM SHAKESPEARE, *TIMON OF ATHENS*

Our hopes, like towering falcons, aim
At objects in an airy height;
The little pleasure of the game
Is from afar to view the flight.

—MATTHEW PRIOR, "TO THE HON. CHARLES MONTAGUE"

I know of only one bird—the parrot—that talks; and
it can't fly very high.

—WILBUR WRIGHT, DECLINING TO MAKE A SPEECH IN 1908

Words are heavy like rocks . . . they weigh you down. If birds could talk, they wouldn't be able to fly.

—MARILYN, CHARACTER ON THE TV SHOW
NORTHERN EXPOSURE

———

Happier of happy though I be, like them
I cannot take possession of the sky,
Mount with a thoughtless impulse, and wheel
   there,
One of a mighty multitude whose way
And motion is a harmony and dance
Magnificent.

—WILLIAM WORDSWORTH, *BIRDS*

Cottleston, Cottleston, Cottleston Pie.
A fly can't bird, but a bird can fly.
Ask me a riddle and I reply:
"Cottleston, Cottleston, Cottleston Pie."

—A. A. MILNE, *WINNIE-THE-POOH*

How do you know but ev'ry Bird that cuts the airy
   way,
Is an immense world of delight,
clos'd by your senses five?

—WILLIAM BLAKE, "THE MARRIAGE OF HEAVEN AND HELL"

Oh, that I had wings like a dove, for then would I fly
away, and be at rest.

—PSALMS 55:6

Science, freedom, beauty, adventure: what more could you ask of life? Aviation combined all the elements I loved. There was science in each curve of an airfoil, in each angle between strut and wire, in the gap of a spark plug or the color of the exhaust flame. There was freedom in the unlimited horizon, on the open fields where one landed. A pilot was surrounded by beauty of earth and sky. He brushed treetops with the birds, leapt valleys and rivers, explored the cloud canyons he had gazed at as a child. Adventure lay in each puff of wind.

I began to feel that I lived on a higher plane than the skeptics of the ground; one that was richer because of its very association with the element of danger they dreaded, because it was freer of the earth to which they were bound. In flying, I tasted a wine of the gods of which they could know nothing. Who valued life more highly, the aviators who spent it on the art they loved, or these misers who doled it out like pennies through their antlike days? I decided that if I could fly for ten years before I was killed in a crash, it would be a worthwhile trade for an ordinary life time.

—CHARLES A. LINDBERGH, *THE SPIRIT OF ST. LOUIS*

No bird soars too high, if he soars with his own wings.

—WILLIAM BLAKE, "PROVERBS OF HELL," *THE MARRIAGE OF HEAVEN AND HELL*

———

Now stagnant grows my too refinéd clay;
I envy birds their wings to fly away.

—JOHN CLARE, "CHILD HAROLD"

Sometimes I feel a strange exhilaration up here which seems to come from something beyond the mere stimulus of flying. It is a feeling of belonging to the sky, of owning and being owned—if only for a moment—by the air I breathe. It is akin to the well known claim of the swallow: each bird staking out his personal bug-strewn slice of heaven, his inviolate property of the blue.

—GUY MURCHIE JR., *SONG OF THE SKY*

You cannot fly like an eagle with the wings of a wren.

—WILLIAM HENRY HUDSON, *AFOOT IN ENGLAND*

To hear the lark begin his flight,
And singing startle the dull night,
From his watch-tower in the skies,
Till the dappled dawn doth rise.

—JOHN MILTON, "L'ALLEGRO"

There is no way to avoid the birds in the air, but the pilots can avoid being where the birds are.

—JEROME A. JACKSON, ON RESEARCHING BIRD MIGRATION TO AVOID AVIATION ACCIDENTS, *THE NEW YORK TIMES*

Parricide (singing): Oh might I but become an eagle who soars in the skies! Oh might I fly above the azure waves of the barren sea!

—ARISTOPHANES, *THE BIRDS*

Faster than a speeding bullet! More powerful than a locomotive! Able to leap tall buildings at a single bound! Look! Up in the sky! It's a bird! It's a plane! It's Superman!

—ANONYMOUS, PREAMBLE TO *SUPERMAN* RADIO SHOW

———•••———

We are all pirates at heart. There is not one of us who hasn't had a little larceny in his soul. And which one of us wouldn't soar if God had thought there was merit in the idea? So, when we see one of those great widespread pirates soaring across the grain of sea winds we thrill, and we long, and, if we are honest, we curse that we must be men every day. Why not one day a bird!

—ROGER CARAS, *BIRDS AND FLIGHT*

All birds that fly have round their leg the thread of
the infinite.

—Victor Hugo, *Les Miserables*, Volume IV, Saint Denis

We have not wings we cannot soar;
But, we have feet to scale and climb,
By slow degrees, by more and more,
The cloudy summits of our time.

—Henry Wadsworth Longfellow,
"The Ladder of St. Augustine"

I think more of a bird with broad wings flying and lapsing through the air, than anything, when I think of metre.

—D. H. LAWRENCE, IN A LETTER TO EDWARD MARSH

You could not see a cloud, because
No cloud was in the sky:
No birds were flying overhead—
There were no birds to fly.

—LEWIS CARROLL, *THROUGH THE LOOKING GLASS*

Cinesias. . . . "I shall travel through thine ethereal empire like a winged bird who cleaveth space with his long neck . . ."

—ARISTOPHANES, *THE BIRDS*

If you are looking for perfect safety, you will do well to sit on a fence and watch the birds; but if you really wish to learn, you must mount a machine and become acquainted with its tricks by actual trial.

—WILBUR WRIGHT

I have known today a magnificent intoxication. I have learnt how it feels to be a bird. I have flown. Yes I have flown. I am still astonished at it, still deeply moved.

—LE FIGARO

The experienced pilot will not make a straight-away glide, but like the vulture, or the condor, and birds of that class, soar in a circle, and thus, by passing over and over the same surfaces of the earth, enable him to select a proper landing place.

—J. S. ZERBE, "EXPERIMENTAL WORKS IN FLYING,"
AEROPLANES, 1915

The time will come, when thou shalt lift thine eyes
To watch a long-drawn battle in the skies.
While aged peasants, too amazed for words,
Stare at the flying fleets of wondrous birds.

England, so long mistress of the sea,
Where winds and waves confess her sovereignty,
Her ancient triumphs yet on high shall bear
And reign the sovereign of the conquered air.

—THOMAS GRAY, "GRAY'S ELEGY"

First, by the figurations of art there be made instruments of navigation without men to row them, as great ships to brooke the sea, only with one man to steer them, and they shall sail far more swiftly than if they were full of men; also chariots that shall move with unspeakable force without any living creature to stir them. Likewise an instrument may be made to fly withall if one sits in the midst of the instrument, and do turn an engine, by which the wings, being artificially composed, may beat the air after the manner of a flying bird.

—FRIAR ROGER BACON

But whether [the source of lift] be a rising current or something else, it is as well able to support a flying machine as a bird, if man once learns the art of utilizing it.

—WILBUR WRIGHT

Lying under an acacia tree with the sound of the dawn around me, I realized more clearly the facts that man should never overlook: that the construction of an airplane, for instance, is simple when compared [with] a bird; that airplanes depend on an advanced civilization, and that where civilization is most advanced, few birds exist. I realized that if I had to choose, I would rather have birds than airplanes.

—CHARLES A. LINDBERGH, INTERVIEW SHORTLY BEFORE HIS DEATH

Birds (General Quotes about Specific Birds)

Look at that mallard as he floats on the lake; see his elevated head glittering with emerald green, his amber eyes glancing in the light! Even at this distance, he has marked you, and suspects that you bear no goodwill towards him, for he sees that you have a gun, and he has many a time been frightened by its report, or that of some other. The wary bird draws his feet under his body, springs upon them, opens his wings, and with loud quacks bids you farewell.

—JOHN JAMES AUDUBON, *THE BIRDS OF AMERICA*

The wild geese were passing over. . . . There was an infinite cold passion in their flight, like the passion of the universe, a proud mystery never to be solved.

—MARTHA OSTENSO, *WILD GEESE*

Let the long contention cease!
Geese are swans, and swans are geese.

—MATTHEW ARNOLD, "THE LAST WORD"

You think that upon the score of fore-knowledge and divining I am infinitely inferior to the swans. When they perceive approaching death they sing more merrily than before, because of the joy they have in going to the God they serve.

—SOCRATES, *IN PHAEDO*

Thinking to get at once all the gold that the goose could give, he killed it, and opened it only to find— nothing.

—AESOP, *FABLES*, "THE GOOSE WITH THE GOLDEN EGGS"

Made poetry a mere mechanic art;
And every warbler has his tune by heart.

—WILLIAM COWPER, "TABLE TALK"

A mocking-bird (*Mimus orpheus*), called by the inhabitants Calandria, is remarkable, from possessing a song far superior to that of any other bird in the country: indeed, it is nearly the only bird in South America which I have observed to take its stand for the purpose of singing.

—CHARLES DARWIN, "THE VOYAGE OF THE BEAGLE"

She was not quite what you would call refined. She was not quite what you would call unrefined. She was the kind of person that keeps a parrot.

—MARK TWAIN, *FOLLOWING THE EQUATOR*

The parrot holds its food for prim consumption as daintily as any debutante, [with] a predilection for pot roast, hashed-brown potatoes, duck skin, butter, hoisin sauce, sesame seed oil, bananas and human thumb.

—ALEXANDER THEROUX, "I SING THE PARROT!" *READER'S DIGEST*

"He is well behaved, senora," the old man said when he sold it to me. "He is not vulgar. He will never embarrass you." The parrot eyed me slyly and malevolently, like a wrongdoer who hears his lawyer praising him in court.

—GERTRUDE DIAMANT, *THE DAYS OF OFELIA*

Four ducks on a pond,
A grass-bank beyond,
A blue sky of spring,
White clouds on the wing:
What a little thing
To remember for years—
To remember with tears!

—WILLIAM ALLINGHAM, "A MEMORY"

And the Raven, never flitting,
Still is sitting, still is sitting
On the pallid bust of Pallas
Just above my chamber door;
And his eyes have all the seeming
Of a demon's that is dreaming,
And the lamplight o'er him streaming
Throws his shadow on the floor,
And my soul from out that shadow,
That lies floating on the floor,
Shall be lifted—nevermore.

—EDGAR ALLAN POE, "THE RAVEN"

Raven from the dim dominions
On the Night's Plutonian shore,
Oft I hear thy dusky pinions
Wave and flutter round my door—
See the shadow of thy pinions
Float along the moonlit floor.

—SARAH HELEN POWER WHITMAN, *THE RAVEN*

Ploffskin, Pluffskin, Pelican jee!
We think no Birds so happy as we!
Plumpskin, Ploshkin, Pelican jill!
We think so then and we thought so still.

—EDWARD LEAR, *NONSENSE SONGS*,
"THE PELICAN CHORUS"

A rare old bird is the pelican;
His bill holds more than his belican.
He can take in his beak
Enough food for a week;
I'm darned if I know how the helican.

—DIXON MERRITT, "THE PELICAN"

If you lie down in a village square hoping to capture a sea gull, you could stay there your whole life without succeeding. But a hundred miles from shore it's different. Sea gulls have a highly developed instinct for self-preservation on land but at sea they're very cocky.

—GABRIEL GARCÍA MÁRQUEZ, THE STORY OF A SHIPWRECKED SAILOR

Most gulls don't bother to learn more than the simplest facts of flight—how to get from shore to food and back again. For most gulls, it is not flying that matters, but eating. For this gull, though, it was not eating that mattered, but flight. More than anything else, Jonathan Livingston Seagull loved to fly.

—RICHARD BACH, *JONATHAN LIVINGSTON SEAGULL*

Remember that the most beautiful things in the world are the most useless; peacocks and lilies, for example.

—JOHN RUSKIN, *THE STONES OF VENICE*

Hail to thee, blithe Spirit!
Bird thou never wert,
That from Heaven, or near it,
Pourest thy full heart
In profuse strains of unpremeditated art.

—Percy Bysshe Shelley, "To a Skylark"

The lark at break of day arising
From sullen earth, sings hymns at heaven's gate.

—William Shakespeare, Sonnet 29

None but the lark so shrill and clear;
How at heaven's gates she claps her wings,
The morn not waking till she sings.

—John Lyly, "Campaspe"

The bisy larke, messager of day.

—GEOFFREY CHAUCER, *CANTERBURY TALES*

I want there to be no peasant in my kingdom so poor that he cannot have a chicken in his pot every Sunday.

—HENRI IV OF FRANCE

I once had a sparrow alight upon my shoulder for a moment, while I was hoeing in a village garden, and I felt that I was more distinguished by that circumstance that I should have been by any epaulet I could have worn.

—HENRY DAVID THOREAU, *WALDEN*

Who killed Cock Robin?
I, said the Sparrow,
With my bow and arrow,
I killed Cock Robin.

Who saw him die?
I, said the Fly,
With my little eye,
I saw him die.

All the birds of the air
Fell a-sighing and a-sobbing,
When they heard the bell toll
For poor Cock Robin.

—"TOMMY THUMB'S PRETTY SONG BOOK"

A nightingale dies for shame if another bird sings better.

—Robert Burton, *The Anatomy of Melancholy*

———

. . . somewhere in the woods beyond the river a nightingale had begun to sing with all the full-throated zest of a bird conscious of having had a rave notice from the poet Keats and only a couple of nights ago a star spot on the programme of the BBC.

—P. G. Wodehouse, *Ring for Jeeves*

All but the wakeful nightingale;
She all night long her amorous descant sung.

—JOHN MILTON, *PARADISE LOST*

Thou wast not born for death, immortal Bird!
No hungry generations tread thee down;
The voice I hear this passing night was heard
In ancient days by emperor and clown:
Perhaps the self-same song that found a path
Through the sad heart of Ruth, when, sick for home,
She stood in tears amid the alien corn;
The same that oft-times hath
Charm'd magic casement, opening on the foam
Of perilous seas, in faery lands forlorn.

—JOHN KEATS, "ODE TO A NIGHTINGALE"

Still are thy pleasant voices, thy nightingales,
  awake;
For Death, he taketh all away, but them he cannot
  take.

—W. J. CORY, "HERACLITUS"

Short, potbellied penguins, whose necks wobbled
with baby fat, huddled together like Russian busi-
nessmen in fur coats.

—DIANE ACKERMAN, *THE MOON BY WHALE LIGHT*

A Mexican newspaper reports that bored Royal Air Force pilots stationed on the Falkland Islands have devised what they consider a marvelous new game. Noting that the local penguins are fascinated by airplanes, the pilots search out a beach where the birds are gathered and fly slowly along it at the water's edge. Perhaps ten thousand penguins turn their heads in unison watching the planes go by, and when the pilots turn around and fly back, the birds turn their heads in the opposite direction, like spectators at a slow-motion tennis match. Then, the paper reports, "The pilots fly out to sea and directly to the penguin colony and overfly it. Heads go up, up, up, and ten thousand penguins fall over gently onto their backs."

—ARTHER "BUGS" BAER

The red-breast whistles from a garden-croft;
And gathering swallows twitter in the skies.

—JOHN KEATS, "TO AUTUMN"

Call for the robin redbreast and the wren,
Since o'er shady groves they hover,
And with leaves and flowers do cover
The friendless bodies of unburied men.

—JOHN WEBSTER

The bird that most impressed me on my walk was the blackbird. I had already heard nightingales in abundance near Lake Como, and had also listened to larks, but I had never heard either the blackbird, the song thrush, or the blackcap warbler; and while I knew that all three were good singers, I did not know what really beautiful singers they were. Blackbirds were very abundant, and they played a prominent part in the chorus which we heard throughout the day on every hand, though perhaps loudest the following morning at dawn. In its habits and manners the blackbird strikingly resembles our American robin, and indeed looks exactly like a robin, with a yellow bill and coal-black plumage. It hops everywhere over the lawns, just as our robin does, and it lives and nests in the gardens in the same fashion. Its song has a general resemblance to that of our robin, but many of the notes are far more musical, more like those of our wood thrush.

Indeed, there were individuals among those we heard certain of whose notes seemed to me almost to equal in point of melody the chimes of the wood thrush; and the highest possible praise for any song-bird is to liken its song to that of the wood thrush or hermit thrush. I certainly do not think that the blackbird has received justice in the books. I knew that he was a singer, but I really had no idea how fine a singer he was. I suppose one of his troubles has been his name, just as with our own cat-bird. When he appears in the ballads as the merle, bracketed with his cousin the mavis, the song thrush, it is far easier to recognize him as the master singer that he is. It is a fine thing for England to have such an asset of the countryside, a bird so common, so much in evidence, so fearless, and such a really beautiful singer.

—THEODORE ROOSEVELT, "OUTDOORS AND INDOORS,"
THEODORE ROOSEVELT: AN AUTOBIOGRAPHY

If I were reincarnated, I'd want to come back a buzzard. Nothing hates him or envies him or wants him or needs him. He is never bothered or in danger, and he can eat anything.

—WILLIAM FAULKNER IN AN INTERVIEW IN
"WRITERS AT WORK'"

Into my field of view runs the oddest-looking creature, a shaggy, pear-shaped fur ball, that sniffs and snorts like an agitated hound.

—DEREK GRZELEWSKI ON THE KIWI BIRD

The song of the canyon wren is the sound of falling water. Its bright tones drop off the canyon rim and fall from ledge to ledge a step at a time, sliding down a pour-off, bouncing onto a sandstone shelf, then dropping to the next layer of stone and down again—a falling scale, eight tones, a liquid octave of birdsong in the hard, sun-cut canyon.

—KATHLEEN DEAN MOORE, *HOLDFAST*, "THE SONG OF THE CANYON WREN"

No sadder sound salutes you than the clear
Wild laughter of the loon.

—CELIA THAXTER, "SEAWARD," *POEMS*

Shoot all the bluejays you want, if you can hit 'em, but remember it's a sin to kill a mockingbird.

—ATTICUS FINCH IN *TO KILL A MOCKINGBIRD* BY HARPER LEE

[The law is like the killy-loo bird, a creature that] insisted on flying backward because it didn't care where it was going but was mightily interested in where it had been.

—FRED RODELL, PROFESSOR OF LAW AT YALE UNIVERSITY IN *THE NEW YORK TIMES*

It was a turkey! He could never have stood upon his legs, that bird! He would have snapped 'em off short in a minute, like sticks of sealing wax.

—CHARLES DICKENS, *A CHRISTMAS CAROL*

Touched by the magic spell, the sacred fountains of
   feeling
Glowed with the light of love, as the skies and
   waters around her.
Then from a neighboring thicket the mocking-bird,
   wildest of singers,
Swinging aloft on a willow spray that hung o'er the
   water,
Shook from his little throat such floods of delirious
   music,
That the whole air and the woods and the waves
   seemed silent to listen.
Plaintive at first were the tones and sad; then
   soaring to madness
Seemed they to follow or guide the revel of frenzied
   Bacchantes.

—HENRY WADSWORTH LONGFELLOW,
EVANGELINE: A TALE OF ACADIE

Not far from Cambridge, close to Trumpington,
Beneath a bridge of stone, there used to run
A brook, and there a mill stood well in view;
And everything I tell you now is true.
Here dwelt a miller many a year and day,
As proud as any peacock, and as gay.

—GEOFFREY CHAUCER, *CANTERBURY TALES*

The flamingoes are the most delicately colored of all the African birds, pink and red like a flying twig of an oleander bush.

—ISAK DINESEN, *OUT OF AFRICA*

We everywhere saw great numbers of partridges (Nothura major). These birds do not go in coveys, nor do they conceal themselves like the English kind. It appears a very silly bird.

—CHARLES DARWIN, "THE VOYAGE OF THE BEAGLE"

Sitting down on a block of granite, it was delightful to watch the various insects and birds as they flew past. The humming-bird seems particularly fond of such shady retired spots.

—CHARLES DARWIN, "THE VOYAGE OF THE BEAGLE"

. . . There through the long, long summer hours,
The golden light should lie,
And thick young herbs and groups of flowers
Stand in their beauty by.
The oriole should build and tell
His love-tale close beside my cell;
The idle butterfly
Should rest him there, and there be heard
The housewife bee and humming-bird . . .

        —WILLIAM CULLEN BRYANT, "JUNE"

I hope you love birds, too. It is economical. It saves going to Heaven.

        —EMILY DICKINSON, IN MARTHA DICKINSON BIANCHI, ED.,
        THE SINGLE HOUND

The song of canaries
Never varies
And when they're molting
They're revolting.

—OGDEN NASH, "THE CANARY," *THE FACE IS FAMILIAR*

A certain red cardinal sounded like a little bottle being filled up, up, up with some clear liquid.

—ELIZABETH ENRIGHT, *GONE-AWAY LAKE*

Two little dicky birds,
Sitting on a wall;
One named Peter,
The other named Paul.
Fly away, Peter!
Fly away, Paul!
Come back, Peter!
Come back, Paul!

—MOTHER GOOSE'S MELODY

All my novels are an accumulation of detail. I'm a bit of a bower-bird.

—PATRICK WHITE

Crows are, as you must know, our most intelligent birds . . . Crows know the value of organization, and are as well drilled as soldiers—very much better than some soldiers, in fact, for crows are always on duty, always at war, and always dependent on each other for life and safety.

—ERNEST THOMPSON SETON, *WILD ANIMALS I HAVE KNOWN,* "SILVERSPOT"

Raptors (Birds of Prey)

The world is grown so bad,
That wrens make prey where eagles dare not perch.

—WILLIAM SHAKESPEARE, *KING RICHARD III*

The eagle suffers little birds to sing.

—WILLIAM SHAKESPEARE, *TITUS ANDRONICUS*

A Nightingale, sitting aloft upon an oak and singing according to his wont, was seen by a Hawk who, being in need of food, swooped down and seized him. The Nightingale, about to lose his life, earnestly begged the Hawk to let him go, saying that he was not big enough to satisfy the hunger of a Hawk who, if he wanted food, ought to pursue the larger birds. The Hawk, interrupting him, said: "I should indeed have lost my senses if I should let go food ready in my hand, for the sake of pursuing birds which are not yet even within sight."

—AESOP, "THE HAWK AND THE NIGHTINGALE"

I wish the bald eagle had not been chosen as the representative of our country; he is a bird of bad moral character; like those among men who live by sharping and robbing, he is generally poor, and often very lousy. The turkey is a much more respectable bird, and withal a true original native of America.

—BENJAMIN FRANKLIN IN A LETTER TO SARAH BACHE ON EAGLES

Eagles: When they walk, they stumble. They are not what one would call graceful. They were not designed to walk. They fly. And when they fly, oh, how they fly, so free, so graceful. They see from the sky what we never see. Steve, you are an eagle.

—INSCRIPTION PRESENTED WITH A PAINTING OF AN EAGLE BY DR. THOMAS C. LEE, PROFESSOR OF SURGERY AT GEORGETOWN UNIVERSITY MEDICAL SCHOOL TO A PARAPLEGIC MEDICAL STUDENT, *THE WASHINGTON POST*

Eagles don't flock—you have to find them one at a time.

—H. ROSS PEROT, TWO-TIME PRESIDENTIAL CANDIDATE FOR THE REFORM PARTY

He clasps the crag with crooked hands;
Close to the sun in lonely lands,
Ringed with the azure world, he stands.
The wrinkled sea beneath him crawls;
He watches from the mountain walls,
And like a thunderbolt he falls.

—LORD TENNYSON, "THE EAGLE"

Eagles may soar, but weasels never get sucked into jet air intakes.

—ANONYMOUS

When thou seest an eagle, thou seest a portion of genius; lift up thy head!

—WILLIAM BLAKE, "PROVERBS OF HELL," *THE MARRIAGE OF HEAVEN AND HELL*

I met a baby owl in a wood, when it fell over dead, apparently from sheer temper, because I dared to approach it. It defied me first, and then died. I have never forgotten the horror and shame I experienced when that soft fluffy thing (towards which I had nothing but the most humanitarian motives) fell dead from rage at my feet.

—VITA SACKVILLE-WEST, "OWLS," *COUNTRY NOTES*

The owl, that bird of onomatopoetic name, is a repetitious question wrapped in feathery insulation especially for winter delivery.

—HAL BORLAND, "QUESTIONER - DECEMBER 27," *SUNDIAL OF THE SEASONS*

———•••••———

Still and silent and inimitably grave, were two baby owls taking an airing. . . . The four eyes were focused like cameras in a certain direction, and anything that came within the line of vision was necessarily taken in by them. One waited with the concentrated longing of the photographed for the little click of release. It never came, and I realized that this was to be an endless exposure.

—MARY WEBB, *THE SPRING OF JOY*

The owl that calls upon the night
Speaks the unbeliever's fright.
He who shall hurt the little wren
Shall never be belov'd by men.

—WILLIAM BLAKE, "AUGURIES OF INNOCENCE"

Such protection as vultures give to lambs.

—RICHARD BRINSLEY SHERIDAN, *PIZARRO*

Silent and deserted was the vine-covered cottage. Smoldering embers marked the site of his great barns. Gone were the thatched huts of his sturdy retainers, empty the fields, the pastures, and corrals. Here and there vultures rose and circled above the carcasses of men and beasts.

—EDGAR RICE BURROUGHS, *TARZAN THE UNTAMED*

Foreign publishers hovered like benevolent vultures over the still-born foetus of the African Muse.

—WOLE SOYINKA, *THE WRITER IN MODERN AFRICA*, "THE WRITER IN A MODERN AFRICAN STATE"

On a summer day, when the great heat induced a general thirst among the beasts, a Lion and a Boar came at the same moment to a small well to drink. They fiercely disputed which of them should drink first, and were soon engaged in the agonies of a mortal combat. When they stopped suddenly to catch their breath for a fiercer renewal of the fight, they saw some Vultures waiting in the distance to feast on the one that should fall first. They at once made up their quarrel, saying, "It is better for us to make friends, than to become the food of Crows or Vultures."

—AESOP, "THE LION AND THE BOAR"

Thou tree of covert and of rest
For this young Bird that is distrest;
Among thy branches safe he lay,
And he was free to sport and play,
When falcons were abroad for prey.

—WILLIAM WORDSWORTH, "SONG AT THE FEAST OF BROUGHAM CASTLE"

As lovely and spare as a falcon swooping.

—*TIME* MAGAZINE ON THOMAS KENEALLY'S *BRING LARKS AND HEROES*

Though ducks fly so fast, and need such good shooting to kill them, yet their rate of speed, as compared to that of other birds, is not so great as is commonly supposed. Hawks, for instance, are faster. Once, on the prairie, I saw a mallard singled out of a flock, fairly overtaken, and struck down, by a large, light-colored hawk, which I supposed to be a lanner, or at any rate one of the long-winged falcons; and I saw a duck hawk, on the coast of Long Island, perform a similar feat with the swift-flying long-tailed duck—the old squaw, or sou'-sou'-southerly, of the baymen.

—THEODORE ROOSEVELT, CHAPTER II, "WATERFOWL," *HUNTING TRIPS OF A RANCHMAN*

A humming bee—a little tinkling rill—
A pair of falcons wheeling on the wing,
In clamorous agitation, round the crest
Of a tall rock, their airy citadel—
By each and all of these the pensive ear
Was greeted, in the silence that ensued,
When through the cottage-threshold we had
    passed,
And, deep within that lonesome valley, stood
Once more beneath the concave of a blue
And cloudless sky.

   —WILLIAM WORDSWORTH, "THE EXCURSION"

Funny Birds/Quips

I never wanted to weigh more heavily on a man than a bird.

—GABRIELLE "COCO" CHANEL, ON WHY SHE NEVER MARRIED
THOSE WITH WHOM SHE WAS INVOLVED,
NY *HERALD TRIBUNE*

───•••───

God gives every bird its food, but he does not throw it into the nest.

—J. G. HOLLAND

Some newspapers are fit only to line the bottom of bird cages.

—SPIRO T. AGNEW, 39TH VICE PRESIDENT OF THE UNITED STATES

In Italy for thirty years under the Borgias they had warfare, terror, murder and bloodshed but they produced Michelangelo, Leonardo da Vinci and the Renaissance. In Switzerland, they had brotherly love; they had five hundred years of democracy and peace and what did they produce? The cuckoo clock.

—ORSON WELLES PLAYING HARRY LIME IN *THE THIRD MAN*

Noise proves nothing. Often a hen who has merely laid an egg cackles as if she has laid an asteroid.

—MARK TWAIN

An author in a Trappist monastery is like a duck in a chicken coop. And he would give anything in the world to be a chicken instead of a duck.

—THOMAS MERTON, QUOTED BY MONICA FURLONG, *MERTON*

It's not pining, it's passed on. This parrot is no more. It's ceased to be. It's expired. It's gone to meet its maker. This is a late parrot. It's a stiff. Bereft of life it rests in peace. It would be pushing up the daisies if you hadn't nailed it to the perch. It's rung down the curtain and joined the choir invisible. It's an ex-parrot.

—JOHN CLEESE, MONTY PYTHON'S FLYING CIRCUS "DEAD PARROT" SKETCH

The Dodo never had a chance. He seems to have been invented for the sole purpose of becoming extinct and that was all he was good for.

—WILL CUPPY, HOW TO BECOME EXTINCT, "THE DODO"

[He] is a tall, grandly built man; [she] tall and deli-
cate. Both are narrow-faced with long, imperial
noses; as they pose for pictures, it is a turkey buzzard sharing companionably with an egret.

—RICHARD EDER ON JACK MANNING'S PHOTOS OF FRANCIS
STEEGMULLER AND SHIRLEY HAZZARD, HUSBAND AND WIFE
WRITERS, "FOR WRITERS, SEPARATE SILENCES," *THE NEW YORK
TIMES*

Beware the Jabberwock, my son!
The jaws that bite, the claws that catch!
Beware the Jubjub bird, and shun
The frumious Bandersnatch!

—LEWIS CARROLL, *THROUGH THE LOOKING GLASS*

The tourists who come to our island take in the Monarchy along with feeding the pigeons in Trafalgar Square.

—WILLIAM HAMILTON, *MY QUEEN AND I*

What's a thousand dollars? Mere chicken feed. A poultry matter.

—GROUCHO MARX

An election is coming. Universal peace is declared, and the foxes have a sincere interest in prolonging the lives of the poultry.

—GEORGE ELIOT, *FELIX HOLT*

Attila the Hen.

—CLEMENT FREUD REFERRING TO MARGARET THATCHER

How monotonous the sounds of the forest would be if the music came only from the Top Ten birds.

—DAN BENNETT

Dead birds don't fall out of their nests.

—WINSTON CHURCHILL, AFTER SOMEONE TOLD HIM THAT THE FLY TO HIS PANTS WAS UNDONE

Many count their chickens before they are hatched; and where they expect bacon, meet with broken bones.

—MIGUEL DE CERVANTES, *DON QUIXOTE*

Why employ intelligent and highly paid ambassadors and then go and do their work for them? You don't buy a canary and sing yourself.

—ALEC DOUGLAS-HOME, FOREIGN SECRETARY OF GREAT BRITAIN, *THE NEW YORK TIMES*

There was an Old Man with a beard,
Who said,"It is just as I feared!—
Two owls and a hen,
Four larks and a wren,
Have all built their nest in my beard!"

—EDWARD LEAR, BOOK OF NONSENSE

When the seagulls are following a trawler, it's because they think sardines are going to be thrown into the sea.

—ERIC CANTONA, AFTER HE KICKED A FAN WHO TAUNTED HIM DURING A SOCCER MATCH, THE INDEPENDENT

The pride of the peacock is the glory of God.
The lust of the goat is the bounty of God.
The wrath of the lion is the wisdom of God.
The nakedness of woman is the work of God.

—WILLIAM BLAKE, "PROVERBS OF HELL"

The mosquito is the state bird of New Jersey.

—ANDY WARHOL

When turkeys mate they think of swans.

—JOHNNY CARSON

A bird in the hand is worth what it will bring.

—AMBROSE BIERCE, *THE DEVIL'S DICTIONARY*

Oh! A private buffoon is a light-hearted loon,
If you listen to popular rumour.

—SIR WILLIAM SCHWENK GILBERT, "THE YEOMEN OF THE GUARD"

There was an old man of Boulogne,
Who sang a most topical song,
It wasn't the words/ Which frightened the birds,
But the horrible double-entendre

—ANONYMOUS

If I didn't start painting, I would have raised chickens.

—GRANDMA MOSES, *GRANDMA MOSES, MY LIFE'S HISTORY*

Since both its national products, snow and chocolate, melt, the cuckoo clock was invented solely in order to give tourists something solid to remember it by.

—ALAN COREN IN REFERENCE TO SWITZERLAND, *THE SANITY INSPECTOR*

Boozer's Revision: A bird in the hand is dead.

—"THE OFFICIAL RULES"

Every cock is proud of his own dunghill.

—THOMAS FULLER, M.D., ON SELF-IMPORTANCE,
GNOMOLOGIA

Magpie, n. A bird whose thievish disposition suggested to someone that it might be taught to talk.

—AMBROSE BIERCE,
THE DEVIL'S DICTIONARY

You have to ask children and birds how cherries and strawberries taste.

—JOHANN WOLFGANG VON GOETHE

Healthy parakeets have the nervous energy of tennis players.

—MIGNON MCLAUGHLIN, *THE SECOND NEUROTIC'S BOO*

———•·•·•———

Penguins mate for life. Which doesn't exactly surprise me that much 'cause they all look alike—it's not like they're gonna meet a better-looking penguin someday.

—ELLEN DEGENERES, COMEDIENNE, IN *MIRABELLA*

———•·•·•———

Who but my father would keep such a bird in a cage?

—HENRY PRINCE OF WALES REFERRING TO SIR WALTER RALEIGH

Did St. Francis preach to the birds? Whatever for? If he really liked birds he would have done better to preach to the cats.

—REBECCA WEST, *THIS REAL NIGHT*

It's true that I did get the girl, but then my grandfather always said, "Even a blind chicken finds a few grains of corn now and then."

—LYLE LOVETT ON MARRYING JULIA ROBERTS

Imagine if birds were tickled by feathers. You'd see a flock of birds come by, laughing hysterically!

—STEVEN WRIGHT, COMEDIAN

Rats with wings.

—WOODY ALLEN, DESCRIBING PIGEONS

Fall is my favorite season in Los Angeles, watching the birds change color and fall from the trees.

—DAVID LETTERMAN

Pigeons on the grass, alas.

—GERTRUDE STEIN

Turkey, n. A large bird whose flesh when eaten on certain religious anniversaries has the peculiar property of attesting piety and gratitude. Incidentally, it is pretty good eating.

—AMBROSE BIERCE, *THE DEVIL'S DICTIONARY*

Many amateurs still think that when birds sing and hop around, they are being merry and affectionate.... I suppose we shall go on regarding this thing as a much loved garden bird, even when it beats on the window with its beak and tells you to get that goddamn food out on the bird table, or else.

—MILES KINGTON, *NATURE MADE RIDICULOUSLY SIMPLE*

Goose, n. A bird that supplies quills for writing. These, by some occult process of nature, are penetrated and suffused with various degrees of the bird's intellectual energies and emotional character, so that when inked and drawn mechanically across by a person called an "author," there results a very fair and accurate transcript of the fowl's thought and feeling. The difference in geese, as discovered by this ingenious method, is considerable: many are found to have only trivial and insignificant powers, but some are seen to be very great geese indeed.

—AMBROSE BIERCE, *THE DEVIL'S DICTIONARY*

As you know, birds do not have sexual organs because they would interfere with flight. As a result,
birds are very, very difficult to arouse sexually. So
when they want to reproduce, birds fly up and stand
on telephone lines.... When they find a conversation
in which people are talking dirty, they grip the line
very tightly until they are both highly aroused, at
which point the female gets pregnant.

—DAVE BARRY, "SEX AND THE SINGLE AMOEBA: WHAT EVERY
TEEN SHOULD KNOW"

I think a cute movie idea would be about a parrot who is raised by eagles. It would be cute because the parrot can't seem to act like an eagle. After a while, though, to keep the movie from getting boring, maybe put in some pornography. Later, we see the happy parrot flying along, acting like an eagle. He sees two parrots below and starts to attack, but it's his parents. Then, some more pornography.

—JACK HANDEY, "DEEP THOUGHTS" FROM *SATURDAY NIGHT LIVE*

A bird in the hand is the best way to eat chicken.

—ANONYMOUS

I know, but this guy doing the flying has no airline experience at all. He's a menace to himself and everything else in the air. . . . Yes, birds too.

—AIR TRAFFIC CONTROLLER IN THE 1980 MOVIE *AIRPLANE*

A bird in the hand may soil your sleeve, but as long as you have got the bird in there, you don't have to worry about where your next meal is coming from.

—FRED ALLEN

A bird in the hand is safer than one overhead.

—ANONYMOUS

Cats may have had their goose
Cooked by tobacco-juice;
Still why deny its use
Thoughtfully taken?

—C. S. CALVERLEY, "ODE TO TOBACCO"

Ostrich, n. A large bird to which (for its sins, doubt-
less) nature has denied that hinder toe in which so
many pious naturalists have seen a conspicuous evidence of design. The absence of a good working
pair of wings is no defect, for, as has been inge-
niously pointed out, the ostrich does not fly.

—AMBROSE BIERCE, THE DEVIL'S DICTIONARY

I have often seen the King consume four plates of different soups, a whole pheasant, a partridge, a large plate of salad, two big slices of ham, a dish of mutton in garlic sauce, a plateful of pastries followed by fruit and hard-boiled eggs. The King and Monsieur greatly like hard-boiled eggs.

—DUCHESS OF ORLÉANS REFERRING TO LOUIS XIV

People think it would be fun to be a bird because you could fly. But they forget the negative side, which is the preening.

—JACK HANDEY, "DEEP THOUGHTS" FROM *SATURDAY NIGHT LIVE*

You can put wings on a pig, but you don't make it an eagle.

—WILLIAM JEFFERSON CLINTON

———•••••———

How come the dove gets to be the peace symbol? How about the pillow? It has more feathers than the dove, and it doesn't have that dangerous beak.

—JACK HANDEY, "DEEP THOUGHTS" *FROM SATURDAY NIGHT LIVE*

———•••••———

Katharine Hepburn's voice:
A cross between Donald Duck and a Stradivarius.

—ANONYMOUS

It's a good thing we have gravity, or else when birds died they'd just stay right up there. Hunters would be all confused.

—STEVEN WRIGHT, COMEDIAN

The black-headed eagle,
As keen as a beagle,
He hunted o'er height and o'er howe,
In the braes o' Gemappe,
He fell in a trap,
E'en let him come out as he dow, dow, dow,
E'en let him come out as he dow.

—ROBERT BURNS, "A TIPPLING BALLAD"

Her voice sounded like an eagle being goosed.

—RALPH NOVAK ON YOKO ONO

Prov*Birds*/Sayings/Advice

Intelligence without ambition is a bird without wings.

—C. Archie Danielson

———•••———

A peacock has too little in its head, too much in its tail.

—Swedish proverb

The country rooster does not crow in the town.

—SWAHILI PROVERB

Before the cock crow twice, thou shalt deny me thrice.

—ST. LUKE 14: 30

With so many roosters crowing, the sun never comes up.

—ITALIAN PROVERB ON ASSISTANCE

If you were born lucky, even your rooster will lay eggs.

—RUSSIAN PROVERB

A wet bird never flies at night.

—ANONYMOUS

When a fowl eats your neighbor's corn, drive it away; another time it will eat yours.

—AFRICAN (OJI) PROVERB

'Tis true; the raven doth not hatch a lark.

—WILLIAM SHAKESPEARE, *TITUS ANDRONICUS*

They that wait upon the Lord shall renew their strength; they shall mount up with wings as eagles.

—ISAIAH 40:31

Though the bird may fly over your head, let it not make its nest in your hair.

—DANISH PROVERB

Better an egg today than a hen tomorrow.

—ANONYMOUS

Eggs and vows are easily broken.

—JAPANESE PROVERB

Even in a golden cage, the nightingale is homesick.

—AMERICAN PROVERB

Go to bed with the lamb, and rise with the lark.

—ANONYMOUS

A Birdcatcher was about to sit down to a dinner of herbs when a friend unexpectedly came in. The bird-trap was quite empty, as he had caught nothing, and he had to kill a pied Partridge, which he had tamed for a decoy. The bird entreated earnestly for his life: "What would you do without me when next you spread your nets? Who would chirp you to sleep, or call for you the covey of answering birds?" The Birdcatcher spared his life, and determined to pick out a fine young Cock just attaining to his comb. But the Cock expostulated in piteous tones from his perch: "If you kill me, who will announce to you the appearance of the dawn? Who will wake you to your daily tasks or tell you when it is time to visit the bird-trap in the morning?" He replied, "What you say is true. You are a capital bird at telling the time of day. But my friend and I must have our dinners." Necessity knows no law.

—AESOP, "THE BIRDCATCHER, THE PARTRIDGE, AND THE COCK"

The moment a little boy is concerned with which is a jay and which is a sparrow, he can no longer see the birds or hear them sing.

—ERIC BERNE, U.S. PSYCHIATRIST, WRITER

The alligator lays eggs but it is not a fowl.

—JAMAICAN PROVERB

The bird of paradise alights only upon the hand that does not grasp.

—JOHN BERRY, *FLIGHT OF WHITE CROWS*

Man is a wingless bird.

—LEBANESE PROVERB

Curses are like chickens; they come home to roost.

—Fourteenth-century Proverb

The law doth punish man or woman
That steels the goose from off the common,
But lets the greater felon loose,
That steels the common from the goose.

—Anonymous, on enclosures during the eighteenth
century

When the cock is drunk, he forgets about the hawk.

—Ashanti Proverb

He is a fool who lets slip a bird in the hand for a bird
in the bush.

—Plutarch, "Of Garrulity"

Those who have high thoughts are ever striving; they are not happy to remain in the same place. Like swans that leave their lake and rise into the air, they leave their home and fly for a higher home.

—THE DHAMMAPADA

Crows are black the whole world over.

—CHINESE PROVERB

If I keep a green bough in my heart, the singing bird will come.

—CHINESE PROVERB

Old proverbe says,
That byrd ys not honest
That fyleth hys owne nest.

—JOHN SKELTON, "POEMS AGAINST GARNESCHE"

A bird in the hand is worth two in the bush.

—LATIN PROVERB

If you cannot catch a bird of paradise, better take a wet hen.

—NIKITA S. KHRUSHCHEV, *TIME* MAGAZINE

Do not scare the birds you are going to shoot.

—MADAGASY PROVERB

The cuckoo comes in April, and stays the month of May; sings a song at midsummer, and then goes away.

—ANONYMOUS

The crow does not roost with the phoenix.

—CHINESE PROVERB

A Tortoise desired to change its place of residence, so he asked an Eagle to carry him to his new home, promising her a rich reward for her trouble. The Eagle agreed, and seizing the Tortoise by the shell with her talons, soared aloft. On their way they met a Crow, who said to the Eagle: "Tortoise is good eating." "The shell is too hard," said the Eagle in reply. "The rocks will soon crack the shell," was the Crow's answer; and the Eagle, taking the hint, let fall the Tortoise on a sharp rock, and the two birds made a hearty meal off the Tortoise. Moral: Never soar aloft on an enemy's pinions.

—AESOP, "THE TORTOISE AND THE BIRDS"

A thousand cranes in the air are not worth one sparrow in the fist.

—EGYPTIAN PROVERB

Sauce for the goose is sauce for the gander.

—ENGLISH PROVERB

Pigs might fly, but they are most unlikely birds.

—NINETEENTH-CENTURY PROVERB

It happened that a Countryman was sowing some hemp seeds in a field where a Swallow and some other birds were hopping about picking up their food. "Beware of that man," quoth the Swallow. "Why, what is he doing?" said the others. "That is hemp seed he is sowing; be careful to pick up every one of the seeds, or else you will repent it." The birds paid no heed to the Swallow's words, and by and by the hemp grew up and was made into cord, and of the cords nets were made, and many a bird that had despised the Swallow's advice was caught in nets made out of that very hemp. "What did I tell you?" said the Swallow. Moral: Destroy the seed of evil, or it will grow up to your ruin.

—AESOP, "THE SWALLOW AND THE OTHER BIRDS"

The bird alighteth not on the spread net when it be-
holds another bird in the snare. Take warning by the
misfortunes of others, that others may not take example from you.

—SAADI

It is a foule byrd that fyleth his owne nest.

—JOHN HEYWOOD, "PROVERBS"

Some Cranes made their feeding grounds on some plowlands newly sown with wheat. For a long time the Farmer, brandishing an empty sling, chased them away by the terror he inspired; but when the birds found that the sling was only swung in the air, they ceased to take any notice of it and would not move. The Farmer, on seeing this, charged his sling with stones, and killed a great number. The remaining birds at once forsook his fields, crying to each other, "It is time for us to be off to Liliput: for this man is no longer content to scare us, but begins to show us in earnest what he can do." If words suffice not, blows must follow.

—AESOP, "THE FARMER AND THE CRANES"

Woe to the house where the hen crows and the rooster is still.

—SPANISH PROVERB

Trumpet in a herd of elephants; crow in the company of cocks; bleat in a flock of goats.

The foxes have holes, and the birds of the air have nests; but the Son of man hath not where to lay his head.

—MATTHEW 8:20

Trumpet in a herd of elephants; crow in the company of cocks; bleat in a flock of goats.

—MALAYAN PROVERB

Parricide (singing): Oh might I but become an eagle who soars in the skies! Oh might I fly above the azure waves of the barren sea!

Pisthetaerus: Ha! It would seem the news was true. I hear someone coming who talks of wings.

Parricide: Nothing is more charming than flying: I am bird-mad and fly toward you, for I want to live with you and obey your laws.

Pisthetaerus: Which laws? The birds have many laws.

Parricide: All of them; but the one that pleases me most is that among the birds it is considered a fine thing to peck and strangle one's father.

Pisthetaerus: Yes, by God! According to us, he who dares to strike his father, while still a chick, is a brave fellow.

Parricide: And therefore I want to dwell here, for I want to strangle my father and inherit his wealth.

Pisthetaerus: But we have also an ancient law written in the code of the storks, which runs thus: "When the stork father has reared his young and has taught them to fly, the young must in their turn support the father."
—ARISTOPHANES, *THE BIRDS*

Birds of a feather will flock together.
—MINSHEU

He that pricketh the eye will make tears to fall;
And he that pricketh the heart maketh it to shew
  feeling.
Whoso casteth a stone at birds frayeth them away;
And he that upbraideth a friend will dissolve
  friendship.
If thou hast drawn a sword against a friend, despair
  not;
For there may be a returning.

—THE WISDOM OF SOLOMON

Old birds are hard to pluck.

—GERMAN PROVERB

Don't count your chickens before they hatch.

—PROVERB

Don't teach your grandmother to suck eggs.

—ANONYMOUS

To kill two birds with one stone.

—SEVENTEENTH-CENTURY PROVERB

To swallow gudgeons ere they're catched, And count their chickens ere they're hatched.

—SAMUEL BUTLER, *HUDIBRAS,* II. III. 923

Suspicions amongst thoughts are like bats amongst birds, they ever fly by twilight.

—FRANCIS BACON, "OF SUSPICION"

A great conflict was about to come off between the Birds and the Beasts. When the two armies were collected together the Bat hesitated which to join. The Birds that passed his perch said: "Come with us"; but he said: "I am a Beast." Later on, some Beasts who were passing underneath him looked up and said: "Come with us"; but he said: "I am a Bird." Luckily at the last moment peace was made, and no battle took place, so the Bat came to the Birds and wished to join in the rejoicings, but they all turned against him and he had to fly away. He then went to the Beasts, but soon had to beat a retreat, or else they would have torn him to pieces. "Ah," said the Bat, "I see now, he that is neither one thing nor the other has no friends."

—AESOP, "THE BAT, THE BIRDS, AND THE BEASTS"

The jay bird don't rob his own nest.

—WEST INDIAN PROVERB

He who hoots with owls by night cannot soar with eagles by day.

—ANONYMOUS

A feather in hand is better than a bird in the air.

—GEORGE HERBERT, "JACULA PRUDENTUM"

He's in great want of a bird that will give a groat for an owl.

—JOHN RAY

No need to teach an eagle to fly.

—GREEK PROVERB

He who is not a bird should not build his nest over abysses.

—NIETZSCHE

Roasted pigeons will not fly into one's mouth.

—DUTCH PROVERB

Do not abstain from sowing for fear of the pigeons.

—FRENCH PROVERB

Be ye therefore wise as serpents, and harmless as doves.

—MATTHEW 10:16

Be ye therefore wise as serpents, and harmless as doves.

God gives every bird his worm, but He does not throw it into the nest.

—P. D. JAMES

Fate is not an eagle, it creeps like a rat.

—ELIZABETH BOWEN

The owl of ignorance lays the egg of pride.

—PROVERB

Live in such a way that you would not be ashamed to sell your parrot to the town gossip.

—WILL ROGERS

As proud as a peacock.

—PROVERB

A parrot is an animal with the ability to imitate man but not enough intelligence to refrain from doing so.

—ANONYMOUS

The partridge loves peas, but not those that go into the pot with it.

—AFRICAN (WOLOF) PROVERB

Byrds of a fether, best flye together.

—GEORGE WHETSTONE

When you soar like an eagle, you attract the hunters.

—MILTON S. GOULD

Laws, like the spider's webs, catch the flies and let the hawk go free.

—SPANISH PROVERB

The turtle lays thousands of eggs without anyone knowing, but when the hen lays an egg, the whole country is informed.

—MALAY PROVERB

Kill not the goose that lays the golden eggs.

—ENGLISH PROVERB

It's a sad house where the hen crows louder than the cock.

—SCOTTISH PROVERB

The owl is small, its screech is loud.

—TAMIL PROVERB

Chicken Little only has to be right once.

—ANONYMOUS

———•✦•———

If you have money, men think you are wise, hand-some, and able to sing like a bird.

—JEWISH PROVERB ON MONEY AND HAPPINESS

———•✦•———

When the fox preaches, look to the geese.

—GERMAN PROVERB

———•✦•———

A Royal Commission is a broody hen sitting on a china egg.

—MICHAEL FOOT TO THE BRITISH PARLIAMENT

Fly and you will catch the swallow.

—JAMES HOWELL, "PROVERBS"

There is no flying without wings.

—FRENCH PROVERB

Feather by feather the goose can be plucked.

—FRENCH PROVERB

Fine feathers make fine birds.

—ENGLISH PROVERB

It is not only fine feathers that make fine birds.

—AESOP, "THE JAY AND THE PEACOCK."

Listen to all, plucking a feather from every passing goose, but, follow no one absolutely.

—CHINESE PROVERB

Three women and a goose make a market.

—PROVERB

The early bird catches the worm.

—WILLIAM CAMDEN

The crow that mimics a cormorant is drowned.

—Japanese Proverb

No need to teach an eagle to fly.

—Greek Proverb

Income taxes transform nest eggs into goose eggs.

—Anonymous

The goose that lays the golden eggs likes to lay where there are eggs already.

—Charles Haddon Spurgeon on ambition

The hunter in pursuit of an elephant does not stop to throw stones at birds.

—UGANDAN PROVERB

You cannot prevent the birds of sorrow from flying over your head, but you can prevent them from building nests in your hair.

—CHINESE PROVERB

Even where there is no cock, day dawns.

—AFRICAN (ZULU) PROVERB

Hongry rooster don't cackle w'en he fine a wum.

—JOEL CHANDLER HARRIS, *UNCLE REMUS: HIS SONGS AND HIS SAYINGS*, "PLANTATION PROVERBS"

Wheresoever the carcass is, there will be eagles gathered together.

—MATTHEW 24:28

All clever men are birds of prey.

—ENGLISH PROVERB

In a group of eagles, you will find some turkeys.

—ANONYMOUS

People live like birds in the woods: When the time comes, each must take flight.

—CHINESE PROVERB

There be three things which are too wonderful for me, yea, four which I know not: The way of an eagle in the air; the way of a serpent upon a rock; the way of a ship in the midst of the sea; and the way of a man with a maid.

—PROVERBS 30, 18–19

The eagle never lost so much time as when he submitted to the learn of the crow.

—WILLIAM BLAKE, "PROVERBS OF HELL," *THE MARRIAGE OF HEAVEN AND HELL*, ON HUMILITY

Eagles do not beget doves.

—PROVERB

An eagle does not catch flies.

—PROVERB

Do not revile the king even in your thoughts, or curse the rich in your bedroom, because a bird of the air may carry your words, and a bird on the wing may report what you say.

—ECCLESIASTES 10:20

Life Lessons from Birds

People expect the clergy to have the grace of a swan, the friendliness of a sparrow, the strength of an eagle and the night hours of an owl—and some people expect such a bird to live on the food of a canary.

—EDWARD JEFFREY, BRITISH CLERGYMAN, *THE NEW YORK TIMES*

—•••—

Use what talents you possess: the woods would be very silent if no birds sang there except those that sang best.

—HENRY VAN DYKE ON TALENT

What is sauce for the goose may be sauce for the gander but is not necessarily sauce for the chicken, the duck, the turkey or the guinea hen.

—ALICE B. TOKLAS, *THE ALICE B. TOKLAS COOKBOOK*

The wild turkey is no sitting duck. . . . It is not a bird to go gently into the roasting pan.

—*THE NEW YORK TIMES*, EDITORIAL

I'm the lamest lame duck there could be.

—GEORGE C. WALLACE, GOVERNOR OF ALABAMA, TO HIS
SUPPORTERS AFTER HIS RETIREMENT AS GOVERNOR

Son, in politics you've got to learn that overnight
chicken shit can turn to chicken salad.

—LYNDON JOHNSON ON POLITICS

Inflation is when sitting on your nest egg doesn't
give you anything to crow about.

—ANONYMOUS

A wise old owl sat on an oak;
The more he saw the less he spoke;
The less he spoke the more he heard;
Why aren't we like that wise old bird?

—EDWARD HERSEY RICHARDS, "A WISE OLD OWL"

Much talking is the cause of danger. Silence is the means of avoiding misfortune. The talkative parrot is shut up in a cage. Other birds, without speech, fly freely about.

—SASKYA PANDITA

Fool that I was, upon my eagle's wings
I bore this wren till I was tired with soaring,
And now he mounts above me.

—JOHN DRYDEN, "ALL FOR LOVE"

All the sparrows on the rooftops are crying about the fact that the most imperialist nation that is supporting the colonial regime in the colonies is the United States of America.

—NIKITA S. KHRUSHCHEV, ADDRESSING THE GENERAL ASSEMBLY

The longer I live, the more convincing proofs I see of this truth: that God governs in the affairs of men. And if a sparrow cannot fall to the ground without His notice, is it probable that an empire can rise without his aid?

—BENJAMIN FRANKLIN, CALLING FOR PRAYER AT THE
CONSTITUTIONAL CONVENTION OF 1787

Birds in their little nests agree;
And 'tis a shameful sight,
When children of one family
Fall out, and chide, and fight.

—ISAAC WATTS, *DIVINE SONGS*

Red: Sometimes it makes me sad though—Andy being gone. I have to remind myself that some birds aren't meant to be caged. Their feathers are just too bright. And when they fly away, the part of you that knows it was a sin to lock them up does rejoice.

—FROM THE MOVIE *THE SHAWSHANK REDEMPTION*

Methinks I see in my mind a noble and puissant nation rousing herself like a strong man after sleep, and shaking her invincible locks. Methinks I see her as an eagle mewing her mighty youth, and kindling her undazzled eyes at the full midday beam.

—JOHN MILTON, "AREOPAGITICA"

I used . . . to keep a book in which I would talk to myself. One of the aphorisms I wrote was, "The structure of a play is always the story of how the birds came home to roost."

—ARTHUR MILLER ON WRITING IN *HARPER'S* MAGAZINE

We have escaped like a bird out of the fowler's snare; the snare has been broken, and we have escaped.

—PSALMS 124:7

An aristocracy in a republic is like a chicken whose head has been cut off: it may run about in a lively way, but in fact it is dead.

—NANCY MITFORD, *NOBLESSE OBLIGE*

America cannot be an ostrich with its head in the sand.

—THOMAS WOODROW WILSON

The only difference between a pigeon and the American farmer is that a pigeon can still make a deposit on a John Deere.

—JIM HIGHTOWER, FORMER TEXAS AGRICULTURE
COMMISSIONER TO CHAMBER OF COMMERCE IN DALLAS,
THE NEW YORK TIMES

I mourn for that most lonely thing; and yet God's will be done:
I knew a phoenix in my youth, so let them have their day.

—W. B. YEATS, *THE WILD SWANS AT COOLE*, "HIS PHOENIX"

I do not believe that any peacock envies another peacock his tail, because every peacock is persuaded that his own tail is the finest in the world. The consequence of this is that peacocks are peaceable birds.

—BERTRAND RUSSELL ON PRIDE, *THE CONQUEST OF HAPPINESS*

The wild goose comes north with the voice of freedom and adventure. He is more than a big, far-ranging bird; he is the epitome of wanderlust, limitless horizons and distant travel. He is the yearning and the dream, the search and the wonder, the unfettered foot and the wind's-will wing.

—HAL BORLAND, "WILD GOOSE - APRIL 8," *SUNDIAL OF THE SEASONS*

The great will not condescend to take any thing seriously; all must be as gay as the song of a canary, though it were the building of cities or the eradication of old and foolish churches and nations which have cumbered the earth long thousands of years.

—RALPH WALDO EMERSON, "HEROISM: AN ESSAY"

So God created the great creatures of the sea and every living and moving thing with which the water teems, according to their kinds, and every winged bird according to its kind. And God saw that it was good.

—GENESIS 1:21

Cheerfulness is proper to the cock, which rejoices over every little thing, and crows with varied and lively movements.

—LEONARDO DA VINCI ON HAPPINESS

He shall purify the house with the bird's blood, the fresh water, the live bird, the cedar wood, the hyssop and the scarlet yarn.

—LEVITICUS 14:52

There are three classes which need sanctuary more than others—birds, wild flowers, and Prime Ministers.

—STANLEY BALDWIN (EARL OF BEWDLEY) ON POLITICS

It's going to come out all right—do you know?
The sun, the birds, the grass—they know.
They get along—and we'll get along.

—CARL SANDBURG FROM "CABOOSE THOUGHTS"

Then he is to release the live bird in the open fields outside the town. In this way he will make atonement for the house, and it will be clean.

—LEVITICUS 14:53

Patriotism is a lively sense of collective responsibility. Nationalism is a silly cock crowing on its own dunghill.

—RICHARD ALDINGTON, *THE COLONEL'S DAUGHTER*

Boredom is the dream bird that hatches the egg of experience. A rustling in the leaves drives him away.

—WALTER BENJAMIN, "THE STORYTELLER"

He prayeth well, who loveth well
Both man and bird and beast.

—SAMUEL TAYLOR COLERIDGE, "THE RIME OF THE ANCIENT MARINER"

The little birds that tune their morning's joy
Make her moans mad with their sweet melody:
For mirth doth search the bottom of annoy;
Sad souls are slain in merry company;
Grief best is pleased with grief's society:
True sorrow then is feelingly sufficed
When with like semblance it is sympathized.

—WILLIAM SHAKESPEARE, "THE RAPE OF LUCRECE"

The sparrow is sorry for the peacock at the burden of his tail.

—RABINDRANATH TAGORE ON CLASS, *STRAY BIRDS*

In the Lord I take refuge. How then can you say to me: "Flee like a bird to your mountain."

—PSALMS 11:1

———

People are crying up the rich and variegated plumage of the peacock, and he is himself blushing at the sight of his ugly feet.

—SA'DI ON IMPERFECTION, *GULISTAN*, TRANSLATED BY JAMES ROSS

A bird appears a thoughtless thing.
No doubt he has his little cares,
And very hard he often fares,
The which so patiently he bears.

—CHARLES LAMB, *CRUMBS TO THE BIRDS*

Come, fill the Cup, and in the Fire of Spring
The Winter Garment of Repentance fling:
The Bird of Time has but a little way
To fly—and Lo! the Bird is on the Wing.

—OMAR KHAYYÁM, "RUBAIYAT OF OMAR KHAYYAM"

When I warned the [the French Government] that Britain would fight on alone whatever they did, their generals told their Prime Minister and his divided Cabinet: "In three weeks England will have her neck wrung like a chicken." Some chicken! Some neck!

—WINSTON CHURCHILL REFERRING TO THE FRENCH GOVERNMENT IN A SPEECH IN THE CANADIAN PARLIAMENT

I shall not ask Jean Jacques Rousseau,
If birds confabulate or no.

—WILLIAM COWPER, "PAIRING TIME ANTICIPATED"

I'd rather learn from one bird how to sing than to
teach ten thousand stars how not to dance.

—E. E. CUMMINGS, "YOU SHALL ABOVE ALL THINGS BE GLAD
AND YOUNG"

The early bird who catches the worm works for someone who comes in late and owns the worm farm.

—TRAVIS MCGEE ON EARLY BIRDS

No bird of prey knows that hidden path, no falcon's eye has seen it.

—JOB 28:7

For man, as for flower and beast and bird, the supreme triumph is to be most vividly, most perfectly alive.

—D. H. LAWRENCE ON LIFE

That was life, she said to herself. Be as cunning as a serpent and as harmless as a dove.

—BUCHI EMECHETA, *SECOND-CLASS CITIZEN*

Hold fast to dreams,
For if dreams die,
Life is a broken-winged bird,
That cannot fly.

—LANGSTON HUGHES, "DREAMS"

The wild deer browse above her breast;
The wild bird raise their brood;
And they, her smiles of love caress'd,
Have left her solitude!

—EMILY BRONTE FROM "MY LADY'S GRAVE"

To live content with small means, to seek elegance rather than luxury, and refinement rather than fashion, to be worthy, not respectable, and wealthy, not rich, to study hard, think quietly, talk gently, act frankly, to listen to stars and birds, to babes and sages, with open heart, to bear all cheerfully, do all bravely, await occasions, hurry never, in a word to let the spiritual, unbidden and unconscious, grow up through the common, this is to be my symphony.

—WILLIAM HENRY CHANNING ON HAPPINESS

I do not know which to prefer,
The beauty of inflections
Or the beauty of innuendoes,
The blackbird whistling
Or just after.

—WALLACE STEVENS, "THIRTEEN WAYS OF LOOKING AT A BLACKBIRD"

A rainbow and a cuckoo's song
May never come together again;
May never come
This side the tomb.

—W. H. DAVIES, "A GREAT TIME"

A bird knows nothing of gladness,
Is only a song machine.

—GEORGE MACDONALD, "A BOOK OF DREAMS"

If the world were so organized that everything has to be fair, no living creature could survive for a day. The birds would be forbidden to eat worms, and everyone's self-interest would have to be served.

—ANONYMOUS ON FAIRNESS

A fox should not be of the jury at a goose's trial.

—THOMAS FULLER ON FAIRNESS

Why should the worm intrude the maiden bud?
Or hateful cuckoos hatch in sparrows' nests?
Or toads infect fair founts with venom mud?
Or tyrant folly lurk in gentle breasts?
Or kings be breakers of their own behests?
But no perfection is so absolute,
That some impurity doth not pollute.

—WILLIAM SHAKESPEARE, "THE RAPE OF LUCRECE"

You don't set a fox to watching the chickens just because he has a lot of experience in the hen house.

—HARRY S. TRUMAN REFERRING TO THE PRESIDENTIAL NOMINATION OF VICE PRESIDENT RICHARD NIXON

Does the Eagle know what is in the pit
Or wilt thou go ask the Mole?
Can Wisdom be put in a silver rod,
Or Love in a golden bowl?

—WILLIAM BLAKE, "THE BOOK OF THEL"

The bird thinks it is an act of kindness to give the fish a lift in the air.

—RABINDRANATH TAGORE ON KINDNESS

Birds of a Feather (Relationships, Family, Friends, Bugs, Zoos, Other Animals, Love, Sex, Marriage)

The season of love is that of battle; but the males of some birds, as of the game-fowl and ruff, and even the young males of the wild turkey and grouse are ready to fight whenever they meet.

— CHARLES DARWIN, *THE DESCENT OF MAN*

Birds of a feather will gather together.

— ROBERT BURTON

Marriage is like a cage; one sees the birds outside desperate to get in, and those inside equally desperate to get out.

— MICHEL DE MONTAIGNE, *ESSAYS*

Almost all male birds are extremely pugnacious, using their beaks, wings, and legs for fighting together. We see this every spring with our robins and sparrows. The smallest of all birds, namely, the humming-bird, is one of the most quarrelsome.

— CHARLES DARWIN, *THE DESCENT OF MAN*

Whether you wind up with a nest egg or a goose egg depends on the kind of chick you married.

—*The Wall Street Journal*

———•-•+•-———

Hot, faint, and weary, with her hard embracing,
Like a wild bird being tamed with too much
handling,
Or as the fleet-foot roe that's tired with chasing,
Or like the froward infant still'd with dandling,
He now obeys, and now no more resisteth,
While she takes all she can, not all she listeth.

—William Shakespeare, "Venus and Adonis"

When you have seen one ant, one bird, one tree, you have not seen them all.

—EDWARD O. WILSON, PROFESSOR OF SCIENCE, HARVARD, ON THE DIFFICULTY OF DISCOVERING NEW PLANTS AND ANIMALS, IN *TIME*

The wild-duck is strictly monogamous, the domestic duck highly polygamous.

—CHARLES DARWIN, *THE DESCENT OF MAN*

. . . but he has brought with him to this house a cockatoo, two canary-birds, and a whole family of white mice. He attends to all the necessities of these strange favourites himself, and he has taught the creatures to be surprisingly fond of him and familiar with him. The cockatoo, a most vicious and treacherous bird towards everyone else, absolutely seems to love him. When he lets it out of its cage, it hops on to his knee, and claws its way up his great big body, and rubs its top-knot against his sallow double chin in the most caressing manner imaginable. He has only to set the doors of the canaries' cages open, and to call them, and the pretty little cleverly trained creatures perch fearlessly on his hand, mount his fat outstretched fingers one by one, when he tells them to "go upstairs," and sing together as if they would burst their throats with delight when they get to the top finger.

—THE COUNT IN WILKIE COLLINS' *THE WOMAN IN WHITE*

It is something—it can be everything—to have found a fellow bird with whom you can sit among the rafters while the drinking and boasting and reciting and fighting go on below.

—WALLACE STEGNER, *THE SPECTATOR BIRD*

Let some cry up woodcock or hare,
Your bustards, your ducks, and your widgeons;
But of all the gay birds in the air,
Here's a health to the Three Jolly Pigeons.

—OLIVER GOLDSMITH, "SHE STOOPS TO CONQUER"

Plato having defined man to be a two-legged animal without feathers, Diogenes plucked a cock and brought it into the Academy, and said, "This is Plato's man." On which account this addition was made to the definition—"with broad at nails."

—DIOGENES LAËRTIUS, *LIVES OF THE PHILOSOPHERS*

Jupiter himself was turned into a satyr, a shepherd, a bull, a swan, a golden shower, and what not for love.

—ROBERT BURTON, *THE ANATOMY OF MELANCHOLY*

A Robin Redbreast in a cage
Puts all Heaven in a Rage.

—WILLIAM BLAKE, "AUGURIES OF INNOCENCE"

The cuckoo then on every tree
Mocks married men, for thus sings he:
"Cuckoo;
Cuckoo, cuckoo"—O word of fear,
Unpleasing to a married ear!

—WILLIAM SHAKESPEARE, *LOVE'S LABOUR'S LOST*

When we behold two males fighting for the possession of the female, or several male birds displaying their gorgeous plumage and performing strange antics before an assembled body of females, we cannot doubt that, though led by instinct, they know what they are about, and consciously exert their mental and bodily powers.

—CHARLES DARWIN, *THE DESCENT OF MAN*

Do not conceive that fine clothes make fine men, any more than fine feathers make fine birds. A plain, genteel dress is more admired, obtains more credit in the eyes of the judicious and sensible.

—GEORGE WASHINGTON

Fowl both of water and land in great plenty and diversity. All kind of green fowl; others as big as bustards, yet not the same. A great white fowl called of some a gaunt. Upon the land divers sort of hawks, as falcons, and others by report. Partridges most plentiful, larger than ours, grey and white of colour, and rough-footed like doves, which our men after one flight did kill with cudgels, they were so fat and unable to fly. Birds, some like blackbirds, linnets, canary birds, and other very small.

—EDWARD HAIES, "SIR HUMPHREY GILBERT'S VOYAGE TO NEWFOUNDLAND"

You shall go with me, newly-married bride,
And gaze upon a merrier multitude.
White-armed Nuala, Aengus of the Birds,
Feachra of the hurtling form, and him
Who is the ruler of the Western Host,
Finvara, and their Land of Heart's Desire.
Where beauty has no ebb, decay no flood,
But joy is wisdom, time an endless song.

—W. B. YEATS, *LAND OF HEART'S DESIRE*

And swans seem whiter if swart crowes be by.

—GUILLAUME DU BARTAS, *DIVINE WEEKES AND WORKES*
"FIRST WEEK, FIRST DAY"

If I shouldn't be alive
When the robins come,
Give the one in red cravat
A memorial crumb.

—EMILY DICKINSON, "TIME AND ETERNITY"

Swamp sparrows, catbird, bluebird, rose-breasted grosbeak, Baltimore oriole, brown thrasher, bobolink, marsh wren, scarlet tanager, indigo bunting hold matins and vespers in the leafy aisles along the brook.

—ELOISE BUTLER, IN MARTHA E. HELLENDER, *THE WILD GARDENER*

I believe no man thinks a goose to be more beautiful than a swan, or imagines that what they call a Friesland hen excels a peacock.

—EDMUND BURKE, "ON TASTE"

I'm waiting for the cock to crow.

—WILLIAM MORRIS HUGHES, IN THE AUSTRALIAN
PARLIAMENT

I think we're a kind of desperation. We're sort of a maddening luxury. The basic and essential human is the woman, and all that we're doing is trying to brighten up the place. That's why all the birds who belong to our sex have prettier feathers—because males have got to try and justify their existence.

—ORSON WELLES

Irks care the crop-full bird? Frets doubt the maw-crammed beast?

—ROBERT BROWNING, *DRAMATIS PERSONAE*, "RABBI BEN EZRA"

The man who said, "A bird in the hand's worth two in the bush" has been putting his bird in the wrong bushes.

—ANONYMOUS

Sparrowhawks, Ma'am.

—THE DUKE OF WELLINGTON, WHEN QUEEN VICTORIA ASKED HIM HOW TO REMOVE SPARROWS FROM THE CRYSTAL PALACE

Like a strange white bird blown out of the frozen
   seas,
Like a bird from the far north blown with a broken
   wing
Into our sooty garden, he drags and beats
From place to place perpetually, seeking release
From me, from the hand of my love which creeps
   up, needing
His happiness, whilst he in displeasure retreats.

       —D. H. LAWRENCE FROM "MONOLOGUE OF A MOTHER"

O lyric Love, half-angel and half-bird
And all a wonder and a wild desire.

—ROBERT BROWNING, *THE RING AND THE BOOK*

———•·•·•———

The bird a nest, the spider a web, man friendship.

—WILLIAM BLAKE, "PROVERBS OF HELL," *THE MARRIAGE OF
HEAVEN AND HELL*

It is often difficult to conjecture whether the many strange cries and notes uttered by male birds during the breeding-season serve as a charm or merely as a call to the female. . . . The spel of the black-cock certainly serves as a call to the female, for it has been known to bring four or five females from a distance to a male under confinement; but as the black-cock continues his spel for hours during successive days, and in the case of the capercailzie "with an agony of passion," we are led to suppose that the females which are present are thus charmed.

—CHARLES DARWIN, *THE DESCENT OF MAN*

Just as man can give beauty, according to his standard of taste, to his male poultry, or more strictly can modify the beauty originally acquired by the parent species, can give to the Sebright bantam a new and elegant plumage, an erect and peculiar carriage—so it appears that female Birds in a state of nature have by a long selection of the more attractive males added to their beauty or other attractive qualities.

—CHARLES DARWIN, *THE DESCENT OF MAN*

Every crow thinks her own bird fairest.

—ROBERT BURTON

Like a bird that strays from its nest is a man who strays from his home.

—PROVERBS 27:8

Birds and Their Surroundings
(Environment, Gardens, Nature, Cities, Weather)

Take any bird, and put it in a cage,
And let your mind and heart alike engage
To serve it tenderly with meat and drink-
All dainty things of which a man can think-
And keep it clean besides in every way;
Although its cage with gold be never so gay,
Yet it would rather, twenty thousand fold,
Live in a forest that is rude and cold,

And feed on worms and other wretched stuff.
For such a bird can never do enough
To get free from its cage, if that may be.
Always it longs to have its liberty.

—GEOFFREY CHAUCER, *CANTERBURY TALES*

The chearful birds their airy carols sing,
And the whole year is one eternal spring.

—OVID, "METAMORPHOSES"

The kiss of sun for pardon,
The song of the birds for mirth—
One is nearer God's Heart in a garden
Than anywhere else on earth.

—DOROTHY GURNEY, "THE LORD GOD PLANTED A GARDEN"

Familiar to everyone. Sooty city birds often bear little resemblance to clean country males with the black throat, white cheeks, chestnut nape.

—ROGER TORY PETERSON, *A FIELD GUIDE TO THE BIRDS : A COMPLETELY NEW GUIDE TO ALL THE BIRDS OF EASTERN AND CENTRAL NORTH AMERICA*

They travel with a constant companion, autumn.

—LARRY VAN GOETHEM, "SOUTHWARD STREAM OF BIRDS OF PREY," *THE NEW YORK TIMES*

———•·•·•———

The season developed and matured. Another year's instalment of flowers, leaves, nightingales, thrushes, finches, and such ephemeral creatures, took up their positions where only a year ago others had stood in their place when these were nothing more than germs and inorganic particles. Rays from the sunrise drew forth the buds and stretched them into long stalks, lifted up sap in noiseless streams, opened petals, and sucked out scents in invisible jets and breathings.

—THOMAS HARDY, *TESS OF THE D'URBERVILLES*

Perfect as the wing of a bird may be, it will never enable the bird to fly if unsupported by the air. Facts are the air of science. Without them a man of science can never rise.

—IVAN PAVLOV

There is nothing in which the birds differ more from man than the way in which they can build and yet leave a landscape as it was before.

—ROBERT LYND, AMERICAN SOCIOLOGIST

Beneath the crisp and wintry carpet hid
A million buds but stay their blossoming
And trustful birds have built their nests amid
The shuddering boughs, and only wait to sing
Till one soft shower from the south shall bid
And hither tempt the pilgrim steps of Spring.

—ROBERT BRIDGES, "THE GROWTH OF LOVE," SONNET VI

At that distant day, when so few men were present to derange the harmony of the wilderness, all the smaller lakes with which the interior of New York so abounds, were places of resort for the migratory aquatic birds; and this sheet, like the others, had once been much frequented by all the varieties of the duck, by the goose, the gull, and the loon.

—JAMES FENIMORE COOPER, *THE DEERSLAYER*

What is more cheerful, now, in the fall of the year, than an open-wood-fire? Do you hear those little chirps and twitters coming out of that piece of apple-wood? Those are the ghosts of the robins and blue-birds that sang upon the bough when it was in blossom last Spring. In Summer whole flocks of them come fluttering about the fruit-trees under the window: so I have singing birds all the year round.

—THOMAS BAILEY ALDRICH, *MISS MEHITABEL'S SON*

Her annual Voiage, born on Windes; the Aire
Floats, as they pass, fann'd with unnumber'd plumes:
From Branch to Branch the smaller Birds with song
Solac'd the Woods, and spred thir painted wings
Till Ev'n, nor then the solemn Nightingal
Ceas'd warbling, but all night tun'd her soft layes:
Others on Silver Lakes and Rivers Bath'd
Thir downie Brest; the Swan with Arched neck
Between her white wings mantling proudly, Rowes
Her state with Oarie feet: yet oft they quit
The Dank, and rising on stiff Pennons, towre
The mid Aereal Skie: Others on ground
Walk'd firm; the crested Cock whose clarion sounds
The silent hours, and th' other whose gay Traine
Adorns him, colour'd with the Florid hue
Of Rainbows and Starrie Eyes. The Waters thus
With Fish replenisht, and the Aire with Fowle,
Ev'ning and Morn solemniz'd the Fift day.

—JOHN MILTON, "PARADISE LOST"

A stage built for public spectacles arranged by Claudius Pulcher won great praise for its painted decoration, because some crows, deceived by a painted representation of roof tiles, tried to alight on them.

—PLINY THE ELDER, *NATURAL HISTORY*

On all the fields round about corn was growing, not only rye and barley, but also oats; yes, the most capital oats, which when ripe, look like a number of little yellow canary birds sitting upon a spray.

—HANS CHRISTIAN ANDERSEN, "THE BUCKWHEAT"

For hours absolute quiet reigned in the little clearing, except as it was broken by the discordant notes of brilliantly feathered parrots, or the screeching and twittering of the thousand jungle birds flitting ceaselessly amongst the vivid orchids and flamboyant blossoms which festooned the myriad, moss-covered branches of the forest kings.

—EDGAR RICE BURROUGHS, *TARZAN OF THE APES*

Tired with their midnight toil, the weary travellers
   slumbered.
Over them vast and high extended the cope of a cedar.
Swinging from its great arms, the trumpet-flower
   and the grapevine
Hung their ladder of ropes aloft like the ladder of
   Jacob,
On whose pendulous stairs the angels ascending,
   descending,
Were the swift humming-birds, that flitted from
   blossom to blossom.

Such was the vision Evangeline saw as she
   slumbered beneath it.
Filled was her heart with love, and the dawn of an
   opening heaven
Lighted her soul in sleep with the glory of regions
   celestial.

> —HENRY WADSWORTH LONGFELLOW, "EVANGELINE: A TALE
> OF ACADIE"

The birds were again skimming the water, or were seen poised on the wing high above the tops of the tallest pines of the mountains, ready to make their swoops, in obedience to the irresistible laws of their nature.

—JAMES FENIMORE COOPER, *THE DEERSLAYER*

On a tree by a river a little tom-tit
Sang "Willow, titwillow, titwillow!"

—W. S. GILBERT, *THE MIKADO*

. . . Bluebirds are gone now,
But they left their song behind them.
The moon seems to say:
It is time for summer when the birds come back
To pick up their lonesome songs.

—HILDA CONKLING, "SNOWFLAKE SONG," *POEMS BY A LITTLE GIRL*

I love the gay Eastertide, which brings forth leaves and flowers; and I love the joyous song of the birds, re-echoing through the copse. But I also love to see, amidst the meadows, tents and pavilions spread; it gives me great joy to see, drawn up on the field, knights and horses in battle array.

—BERTRAN DE BORN, FRENCH SOLDIER AND TROUBADOUR

The bird seeks the tree, not the tree the bird.

—MEXICAN PROVERB

The principality of the sky lightens now, over our green hill, into spring morning larked and crowed and belling.

—DYLAN THOMAS, WELSH POET, SHORT-STORY WRITER AND PLAYWRIGHT

These are brand new birds of twelve-months'
   growing,
Which a year ago, or less than twain,
No finches were, nor nightingales,
Nor thrushes,
But only particles of grain,
And earth, and air, and rain.

—THOMAS HARDY, *PROUD SONGSTERS*

This is the weather the cuckoo likes,
And so do I;
When showers betumble the chestnut spikes,
And nestlings fly:
And the little brown nightingale bills his best,
And they sit outside at "The Travellers' Rest".

—THOMAS HARDY, *LATE LYRICS AND EARLIER* "WEATHERS"

The owl, night's herald, shrieks, 'Tis very late;
The sheep are gone to fold, birds to their nest,
And coal-black clouds that shadow heaven's light
Do summon us to part and bid good night.

—WILLIAM SHAKESPEARE, *VENUS AND ADONIS*

He was like a cock who thought the sun had risen
to hear him crow.

—GEORGE ELIOT, *ADAM BEDE*

But when the birds are gone, and their warm fields
Return no more, where, then, is paradise?

—WALLACE STEVENS, "SUNDAY MORNING"

The Saurophagus sulphuratus is typical of the great American tribe of tyrant-flycatchers. In its structure it closely approaches the true shrikes, but in its habits may be compared to many birds. I have frequently observed it, hunting a field, hovering over one spot like a hawk, and then proceeding on to another. When seen thus suspended in the air, it might very readily at a short distance be mistaken for one of the Rapacious order; its stoop, however, is very inferior in force and rapidity to that of a hawk. At other times the Saurophagus haunts the neighbourhood of water, and there, like a kingfisher, remaining stationary, it catches any small fish which may come near the margin. These birds are not unfrequently kept either in cages or in courtyards, with their wings cut. They soon become tame, and are very amusing from their cunning odd manners, which were described to me as being similar to those of the common magpie. Their flight is undulatory, for the weight of the head and bill appears too great for the body.

—CHARLES DARWIN, "THE VOYAGE OF THE BEAGLE"

Of such therefore as are bred in our land, we have the crane, the bitter, the wild and tame swan, the bustard, the heron, curlew, snite, wildgoose, wind or doterell, brant, lark, plover (of both sorts), lapwing, teal, widgeon, mallard, sheldrake, shoveller, pee-witt, seamew, barnacle, quail (who, only with man, are subject to the falling sickness), the knot, the oliet or olive, the dunbird, woodcock, partridge, and pheasant, besides divers others, whose names to me are utterly unknown, and much more the taste of their flesh, wherewith I was never acquainted.

—WILLIAM HARRISON ON BIRDS IN ENGLAND, *DESCRIPTION OF ELIZABETHAN ENGLAND*, CHAPTER XIII

The thousands of warblers and thrushes, the richly blossoming magnolias, the holly, beech, tall yellow poplar, red clay earth, and hilly ground delighted any eye.

—JOHN JAMES AUDUBON ON VISITING OAKLEY FARM IN LOUISIANA, *JOURNAL*

At some moment in September when there is an intimation of fall—perhaps a certain slant of light across the browning meadow in the hush of a late afternoon when the wind from the sea has suddenly died—I think of the fiercely independent ruffed grouse, a game bird without peer.

—NELSON BRYANT, "GROUSE HUNTING HAS ITS RITUAL," *THE NEW YORK TIMES*

When icicles hang by the wall,
And Dick the shepherd blows his nail,
And Tom bears logs into the hall,
And milk comes frozen home in pail,
When blood is nipp'd, and ways be foul,
Then nightly sings the staring owl:
"Tu-who;
Tu-whit, Tu-who"—A merry note,
While greasy Joan doth keel the pot.

—WILLIAM SHAKESPEARE, *LOVE'S LABOUR'S LOST*

No shade, no shine, no butterflies, no bees,
No fruits, no flowers, no leaves, no birds,—
    November!

—THOMAS HOOD, "NO!"

Ah, sad and strange as in dark summer dawns
The earliest pipe of half-awakened birds
To dying ears, when unto dying eyes
The casement slowly grows a glimmering square;
So sad, so strange, the days that are no more.

—LORD ALFRED TENNYSON, "THE PRINCESS"

Save that from yonder ivy-mantled tow'r
The moping owl does to the moon complain.

—THOMAS GRAY, "ELEGY WRITTEN IN A COUNTRY
CHURCH-YARD"

The number of beautiful fishing birds, such as egrets and cranes, and the succulent plants assuming most fantastical forms, gave to the scene an interest which it would not otherwise have possessed.

—CHARLES DARWIN, "THE VOYAGE OF THE BEAGLE"

The poetry of earth is never dead:
When all the birds are faint with the hot sun,
And hide in cooling trees, a voice will run
From hedge to hedge about the new-mown mead.

—JOHN KEATS, SONNET, ON THE GRASSHOPPER AND CRICKET

The screech and mechanical uproar of the big city turns the citified head, fills citified ears—as the song of birds, wind in the trees, animal cries, or as the voices and songs of his loved ones once filled his heart. He is sidewalk-happy.

—FRANK LLOYD WRIGHT, *THE LIVING CITY*, "EARTH"

Nothing wholly admirable ever happens in this country except the migration of birds.

—BROOKS ATKINSON, "MARCH 23," *ONCE AROUND THE SUN*

One swallow does not make a summer, but one skein of geese, cleaving the murk of March thaw, is the Spring.

—ALDO LEOPOLD, *A SAND COUNTY ALMANAC*

How pleasant the lives of the birds must be,
Living in love in a leafy tree!

—MARY HOWITT, "BIRDS IN SUMMER," *BALLADS AND OTHER POEMS*

It was one of those perfect summer days—the sun was shining, a breeze was blowing, the birds were singing, and the lawn mower was broken.

—JAMES DENT, IN THE CHARLESTON, WEST VIRGINIA, *GAZETTE*

———◆·◆·◆———

The first robin, the first bluebird, the first song sparrow, the first phoebe, the first swallow, is an event which we mention to our neighbor, or write in our letters to our friends. It is an old story with a new interest. The birds have lived, and we have lived to meet again the old scenes. They bring us once more the assurance of the unfailing return of spring, and the never-ending joy and fecundity of life.

—JOHN BURROUGHS, "THE FAMILIAR BIRDS"

It is a city where you can see a sparrow fall to the ground, and God watching it.

—CONOR CRUISE O'BRIEN IN REFERENCE TO DUBLIN

By shallow rivers, to whose falls,
Melodious birds sing madrigals.

—CHRISTOPHER MARLOWE, "THE PASSIONATE SHEPHERD TO HIS LOVE"

For many birds May is the most important month of the year, for it is their time of nesting. Their song now approaches its greatest perfection. Early in the month it expresses the rapture of courtship, later the joy of possession.

—MRS. WILLIAM STARR DANA, ACCORDING TO SEASON

Over increasingly large areas of the United States, spring now comes unheralded by the return of the birds, and the early mornings are strangely silent where once they were filled with the beauty of bird song.

—RACHEL CARSON, *SILENT SPRING*

That man's best works should be such bungling imitations of Nature's infinite perfection, matters not much; but that he should make himself an imitation, this is the fact which Nature moans over, and deprecates beseechingly. Be spontaneous, be truthful, be free, and thus be individuals! is the song she sings through warbling birds, and whispering pines, and roaring waves, and screeching winds.

—LYDIA MARIA CHILD, *LETTERS FROM NEW YORK*

The Body of the Bird
(Aging, Youth, Health and Medicine, Feathers, Hunting, and Eating)

I never saw any other bird where the force of its wings appeared (as in a butterfly) so powerful in proportion to the weight of its body. When hovering by a flower, its tail is constantly expanded and shut like a fan, the body being kept in a nearly vertical position. This action appears to steady and support the bird, between the slow movements of its wings.

—CHARLES DARWIN ON HUMMINGBIRDS, "THE VOYAGE OF THE BEAGLE"

There was an Old Man who said, "Hush!
I perceive a young bird in this bush!"
When they said, "Is it small?"
He replied, "Not at all!
It is four times as big as the bush!"

—EDWARD LEAR, "THE OLD MAN WHO SAID 'HUSH!'"

And wherever you live, you must not eat the blood
of any bird or animal.

—LEVITICUS 7:26

The woodcock is a living refutation of the theory that the utility of a game bird is to serve as a target, or to pose gracefully on a slice of toast. No one would rather hunt woodcock in October than I, but since learning of the sky dance I find myself calling one or two birds enough. I must be sure that, come April, there be no dearth of dancers in the sunset sky.

—ALDO LEOPOLD, *A SAND COUNTY ALMANAC*

A dear old man with his bald pate and spectacles, beaky nose and birdlike lips and benign but somewhat toothless smile.

—RODNEY BENNETT ON MAHATMA GANDHI

Like a young eagle, who has lent his plume
To fledge the shaft by which he meets his doom,
See their own pluck'd to wing the dart
Which rank corruption destines for their heart.

—THOMAS MOORE, "CORRUPTION"

The day is done, and the darkness
Falls from the wings of Night,
As a feather is wafted downward
From an eagle in his flight.

—HENRY WADSWORTH LONGFELLOW, "DAY IS DONE"

Jupiter determined, it is said, to create a sovereign over the birds, and made proclamation that on a certain day they should all present themselves before him, when he would himself choose the most beautiful among them to be king. The Jackdaw, knowing his own ugliness, searched through the woods and fields, and collected the feathers which had fallen from the wings of his companions, and stuck them in all parts of his body, hoping thereby to make himself the most beautiful of all. When the appointed day arrived, and the birds had assembled before Jupiter, the Jackdaw also made his appearance in his many feathered finery. But when Jupiter proposed to make him king because of the beauty of his plumage, the birds indignantly protested, and each plucked from him his own feathers, leaving the Jackdaw nothing but a Jackdaw.

—AESOP, "THE VAIN JACKDAW"

So the struck eagle, stretch'd upon the plain,
No more through rolling clouds to soar again,
View'd his own feather on the fatal dart,
And wing'd the shaft that quiver'd in his heart.

—LORD BYRON, *ENGLISH BARDS AND SCOTCH REVIEWERS*

The same hour was the thing fulfilled upon Nebuchadnezzar: and he was driven from men, and did eat grass as oxen, and his body was wet with the dew of heaven, till his hairs were grown like eagles' feathers, and his nails like birds' claws.

—DANIEL 4:33

The occupation of part of my time in fishing and fowling had frequently tended to preserve me from falling into hurtful associations; but through the rising intimations and reproofs of divine grace in my heart, I now began to feel that the manner in which I sometimes amus'd myself with my gun was not without sin; for although I mostly preferr'd going alone, and while waiting in stillness for the coming of the fowl, my mind was at times so taken up in divine meditations, that the opportunities were seasons of instruction and comfort to me; yet, on other occasions, when accompanied by some of my acquaintances, and when no fowls appear'd which would be useful to us after being obtain'd, we sometimes, from wantonness or for mere diversion, would destroy the small birds which could be of no service to us. This cruel procedure affects my heart while penning these lines.

—WALT WHITMAN, "NOTES (SUCH AS THEY ARE) FOUNDED ON ELIAS HICKS"

A lot of Thanksgiving days have been ruined by not carving the turkey in the kitchen.

—KIN HUBBARD

What a cunning mixture of sentiment, pity, tenderness, irony surrounds adolescence, what knowing watchfulness! Young birds on their first flight are hardly so hovered around.

—GEORGES BERNANOS, *DIARY OF A COUNTRY PRIEST*

Of birds, two species of the genus Pteroptochos (megapodius and albicollis of Kittlitz) are perhaps the most conspicuous. The former, called by the Chilenos "el Turco," is as large as a fieldfare, to which bird it has some alliance; but its legs are much longer, tail shorter, and beak stronger: its colour is a reddish brown. The Turco is not uncommon. It lives on the ground, sheltered among the thickets which are scattered over the dry and sterile hills. With its tail erect, and stilt-like legs, it may be seen every now and then popping from one bush to another with uncommon quickness. It really requires little imagination to believe that the bird is ashamed of itself, and is aware of its most ridiculous figure. On first seeing it, one is tempted to exclaim "A vilely stuffed specimen has escaped from some museum, and has come to life again!" It cannot be made to take flight without the greatest trouble, nor does it run, but only hops. The various loud cries which it utters when concealed amongst the bushes, are as strange as its appearance. It is said to build its nest in a deep hole beneath the ground. I dissected several specimens: the gizzard, which was very muscular, contained beetles, vegetable fibres, and pebbles. From this character, from the length of its legs, scratching feet, membranous covering to the nostrils, short and arched wings, this bird seems in a certain degree to connect the thrushes with the gallinaceous order.

—CHARLES DARWIN, "THE VOYAGE OF THE BEAGLE"

Birds in their little nests agree
With Chinamen, but not with me.

—HILAIRE BELLOC, "ON FOOD"

Society, friendship, and love,
Divinely bestowed upon man,
Oh, had I the wings of a dove,
How soon would I taste you again!

—WILLIAM COWPER, "THE SOLITUDE OF ALEXANDER
SELKIRK"

As wicked dew as e'er my mother brush'd
With raven's feather from unwholesome fen,
Drop on you both! a south-west blow on ye,
And blister you all o'er!

—WILLIAM SHAKESPEARE, *THE TEMPEST*

Even as an empty eagle, sharp by fast,
Tires with her beak on feathers, flesh and bone,
Shaking her wings, devouring all in haste,
Till either gorge be stuff'd or prey be gone:
Even so she kiss'd his brow, his cheek, his chin,
And where she ends she doth anew begin.

—WILLIAM SHAKESPEARE, *VENUS AND ADONIS*

"God save thee, ancient Mariner!
From the fiends that plague thee thus!—
Why look'st thou so?"—With my cross-bow
I shot the Albatross.

—SAMUEL TAYLOR COLERIDGE, "THE RIME OF THE ANCIENT MARINER"

"Of course you know that was the most exquisite sight I ever saw," she said. "I never shall forget it. I did not think there were that many different birds in the whole world. Of all the gaudy colours! And they came so close you could have reached out and touched them."

"Yes," said the Harvester calmly. "Birds are never afraid of me. At Medicine Woods, when I call them like that, many, most of them, in fact, eat from my hand. If you ever have looked at me enough to notice bulgy pockets, they are full of wheat. These birds are strangers, but I'll wager you that in a week I can make them take food from me. Of course, my own birds know me, because they are around every day. It is much easier to tame them in winter, when the snow has fallen and food is scarce, but it only takes a little while to win a bird's confidence at any season."

"Birds don't know what there is to be afraid of," she said.

"Your pardon," said the Harvester, "but I am familiar with them, and that is not correct. They have more to fear than human beings. No one is going to kill you merely to see if he can shoot straight enough to hit. Your life is not in danger because you have magnificent hair that some woman would like for an ornament. You will not be stricken out in a flash because there are a few bits of meat on your frame some one wants to eat. No one will set a seductive trap for you, and, if you are tempted to enter it, shut you from freedom and natural diet, in a cage so small you can't turn around without touching bars. You are in a secure and free position compared with the birds. I also have observed that they know guns, many forms of traps, and all of them decide by the mere manner of a man's passing through the woods whether he is a friend or an enemy. Birds know more than many people realize. They do not always correctly estimate gun range, they are fool-ishly venturesome at times when they want food, but they know many more things than most people give them credit for understanding. The greatest trouble with the birds is they are too willing to trust us and be friendly, so they are often deceived."

—GENE STRATTON PORTER, "THE CHIME OF THE BLUE BELLS," *THE HARVESTER*

He carried his childhood like a hurt warm bird held to his middle-aged breast.

—HERBERT GOLD, *THE AGE OF HAPPY PROBLEMS*

Half of the modern drugs could well be thrown out of the window, except that the birds might eat them.

—MARTIN HENRY FISCHER, MD

The birds are moulting. If only man could moult also—his mind once a year its errors, his heart once a year its useless passions.

—JAMES ALLEN, *A KENTUCKY CARDINAL*

———

The humming-bird, both in shape and colouring, yields to none of the winged species, of which it is the least; and perhaps his beauty is enhanced by his smallness. But there are animals, which, when they are extremely small, are rarely (if ever) beautiful.

—EDMUND BURKE, *SUBLIME AND BEAUTIFUL*

When you have shot one bird flying you have shot all birds flying. They are all different and they fly in different ways but the sensation is the same and the last one is as good as the first.

—ERNEST HEMINGWAY, *WINNER TAKE NOTHING*

You may eat any clean bird.

—DEUTERONOMY 14:11

MACBETH: The devil damn thee black, thou
    cream-faced loon!
Where gott'st thou that goose look?

—WILLIAM SHAKESPEARE, *MACBETH*

The swan, confessedly a beautiful bird, has a neck longer than the rest of his body, and but a very short tail: is this a beautiful proportion? We must allow that it is. But then what shall we say to the peacock, who has comparatively but a short neck, with a tail longer than the neck and the rest of the body taken together? How many birds are there that vary infinitely from each of these standards, and from every other which you can fix; with proportions different, and often directly opposite to each other! and yet many of these birds are extremely beautiful; when upon considering them we find nothing in any one part that might determine us, a priori, to say what the others ought to be, nor indeed to guess anything about them, but what experience might show to be full of disappointment and mistake.

—EDMUND BURKE, *SUBLIME AND BEAUTIFUL*

O thrush, your song is passing sweet,
But never a song that you have sung
Is half so sweet as thrushes sang
When my dear love and I were young.

—WILLIAM MORRIS, "OTHER DAYS"

Measure your health by your sympathy with morning and spring. If there is no response in you to the
awakening of nature—if the prospect of an early
morning walk does not banish sleep, if the warble of
the first bluebird does not thrill you—know that the
morning and spring of your life are past. Thus may
you feel your pulse.

—HENRY DAVID THOREAU, JOURNALS

. . . But the Raven, sitting lonely on the placid bust, spoke only
That one word, as if his soul in that one word he did outpour.
Nothing farther then he uttered—not a feather then he fluttered—
Till I scarcely more than muttered "Other friends have flown before—
On the morrow he will leave me, as my hopes have flown before."
Then the bird said "Nevermore." . . .

—EDGAR ALLAN POE, "THE RAVEN"

Seven to eleven is a huge chunk of life, full of dulling and forgetting. It is fabled that we slowly lose the gift of speech with animals, that birds no longer visit our windowsills to converse. As our eyes grow accustomed to sight they armour themselves against wonder.

—LEONARD COHEN

It is called Tapacolo, or "cover your posterior;" and well does the shameless little bird deserve its name; for it carries its tail more than erect, that is, inclined backwards towards its head . . . The Tapacolo is very crafty: when frightened by any person, it will remain motionless at the bottom of a bush, and will then, after a little while, try with much address to crawl away on the opposite side. It is also an active bird, and continually making a noise: these noises are various and strangely odd; some are like the cooing of doves, others like the bubbling of water, and many defy all similes. The country people say it changes its cry five times in the year—according to some change of season, I suppose.

—CHARLES DARWIN, "THE VOYAGE OF THE BEAGLE"

The tuft of hair on the breast of the wild turkey cock cannot be of any use, and it is doubtful whether it can be ornamental in the eyes of the female bird; indeed, had the tuft appeared under domestication, it would have been called a monstrosity.

—CHARLES DARWIN, *ORIGIN OF SPECIES*

Bird Watching

With one eye on the bird, and the other on the Girl sitting in amazed silence, the Harvester began working for effect. He lay quietly, but in turn he answered a dozen birds so accurately they thought their mates were calling, and closer and closer they came. An oriole in orange and black heard his challenge, and flew up the river bank, answering at steady intervals for quite a time before it was visible, and in resorting to the last notes he could think of, a quail whistled "Bob White" and a shitepoke, skulking along the river bank, stopped and cried, "Cowk, cowk!"

At his limit of calls the Harvester changed his notes and whistled and cried bits of bird talk in tone with every mellow accent and inflection he could manage. Gradually the excitement subsided, the birds flew and tilted closer, turned their sleek heads, peered with bright eyes, and ventured on and on until the very bravest, the wren and the jay, were almost in touch. Then, tired of hunting, Belshazzar came racing and the little feathered people scattered in precipitate flight.

—GENE STRATTON PORTER, "THE CHIME OF THE BLUE BELLS," *THE HARVESTER*

Like dogs in a wheel, birds in a cage, or squirrels in a chain, ambitious men still climb and climb, with great labor, and incessant anxiety, but never reach the top.

—ROBERT BURTON

. . . For there I picked up on the heather
And there I put inside my breast

A moulted feather, an eagle-feather!
Well, I forget the rest.

—ROBERT BROWNING, "MEMORABILIA"

Second-hand are wild books, homeless books; they have come together in vast flocks of variegated feather, and have a charm which the domesticated volumes of the library lack.

—VIRGINIA WOOLF, *THE ART OF THE PERSONAL ESSAY*

I lie awake; I have become like a bird alone on a roof.

—PSALMS 102:7

It's hard to tell the purpose of a bird;
For relevance it does not seem to try.
No line can trace, no flute exemplify
Its traveling; it darts without the word.
Who will devoutly to absorb, contain,
Birds give him pain.

—RICHARD WILBUR, "IN A BIRD SANCTUARY"

———

We carry our homes within us which enables us to fly.

—JOHN CAGE

———

A good servant is a real godsend, but truly this is a rare bird in the land.

—MARTIN LUTHER

A bird on the wing is not so beautiful as when it is perched; nay, there are several of the domestic fowls which are seldom seen to fly, and which are nothing the less beautiful on that account; yet birds are so extremely different in their form from the beast and human kinds, that you cannot, on the principle of fitness, allow them anything agreeable, but in consideration of their parts being designed for quite other purposes.

—EDMUND BURKE, *SUBLIME AND BEAUTIFUL*

Who is this rare bird, perched at the eerie dead center of the world's hurricane, whom all men delight to praise? A Machiavelli with a Boy Scout's exterior? A gross flatterer? A Talleyrand subtler than Khrishna Menon? A monstrous appeaser? Clean is the word for Hammarskjöld.

—ALISTAIR COOKE, ON DAG HAMMARSKJÖLD, NY *HERALD TRIBUNE*

Poetry is like a bird, it ignores all frontiers.

—YEVGENY ALEKSANDROVICH YEVTUSHENKO, *QUOTE*

There were three ravens sat on a tree,
They were as black as they might be.
The one of them said to his make,
"Where shall we our breakfast take?"

—ANONYMOUS, "THE THREE RAVENS"

A wise old owl sat upon an oak
The more he saw the less he spoke
The less he spoke the more he heard
Why aren't we like that wise old bird?

—EDWARD HERSEY RICHARDS, "A WISE OLD OWL"

The silence and the solitude were touched by wild music, thin as air, the faraway gabbling of geese flying at night. Presently I caught sight of them as they streamed across the face of the moon, the high, excited clamor of their voices tingling through the night, and suddenly I saw, in one of those rare moments of insight, what it means to be wild and free.

—MARTHA REBEN, *A SHARING OF JOY*

The very idea of a bird is a symbol and a suggestion to the poet. A bird seems to be at the top of the scale, so vehement and intense his life. . . . The beautiful vagabonds, endowed with every grace, masters of all climes, and knowing no bounds— how many human aspirations are realised in their free, holiday-lives—and how many suggestions to the poet in their flight and song!

—JOHN BURROUGHS, *BIRDS AND POETS*

Take any bird and put it in a cage
And do your best affection to engage
And rear it tenderly with meat and drink
Of all the dainties that you can bethink,
And always keep it cleanly as you may;
Although its cage of gold be never so gay,
Yet would this bird, by twenty thousand-fold,
Rather, within a forest dark and cold,
Go to eat worms and all such wretchedness.

—GEOFFREY CHAUCER, "THE MANCIPLE'S TALE"

Or like stout Cortez when with eagle eyes
He star'd at the Pacific—and all his men
Look'd at each other with a wild surmise—
Silent, upon a peak in Darien.

—JOHN KEATS, "ON FIRST LOOKING INTO CHAPMAN'S
HOMER"

She was one of the early birds,
And I was one of the worms.

> —T. W. CONNOR, "SHE WAS A DEAR LITTLE DICKIE-BIRD"

We think caged birds sing, when indeed they cry.

> —JOHN WEBSTER, "A LAND DIRGE"

'Tis just like a summer bird-cage in a garden—the birds that are without despair to get in, and the birds that are within despair and are in consumption for fear they shall never get out.

> —JOHN WEBSTER, "THE WHITE DEVIL"

The caged bird sings
with a fearful trill
of things unknown
but the longed for still . . .
. . . the caged bird
sings of freedom.

> —MAYA ANGELOU, "CAGED BIRD," PUBLISHED IN *SHAKER,*
> *WHY DON'T YOU SING?*

All his own geese are swans, as the swans of others
are geese.

> —HORACE WALPOLE ABOUT SIR JOSHUA REYNOLDS IN A
> LETTER TO ANNE, COUNTESS OF UPPER OSSORY

In order to understand birds
You have to be a convict.
And if you share your bread—
It means your time is done.

—IRINA RATUSHINSKAYA, "THE SPARROWS OF BUTYRKI,"
PUBLISHED IN *NO, I'M NOT AFRAID*

For most bird-watchers, the coming of the warblers
has the same effect as catnip on a cat.

—ARLINE THOMAS, IN *AUDUBON'S BIRDS*

Little islands are all large prisons: one cannot look
at the sea without wishing for the wings of a swallow.

—SIR RICHARD BURTON, *WANDERINGS IN WEST AFRICA*

I think we consider too much the good luck of the early bird, and not enough the bad luck of the early worm.

—Franklin Delano Roosevelt

To a man, ornithologists are tall, slender, and bearded so that they can stand motionless for hours, imitating kindly trees, as they watch for birds.

—Gore Vidal, *Armageddon? Essays 1983–1987*, "Mongolia!"

Few forms of life are so engaging as birds.

—Ellen Glasgow, *Letters of Ellen Glasgow*

Birds! birds! ye are beautiful things,
With your earth-treading feet and your cloud-
   cleaving wings!
   —Eliza Cook, "Birds"

Birds and beasts have in fact our own nature, flat-
tened a semi-tone.
   —Lydia Maria Child, *Letters From New York*, 2nd
   series

But we, how shall we turn to little things
And listen to the birds and winds and streams
Made holy by their dreams,
Nor feel the heart-break in the heart of things?

    —WILFRID WILSON GIBSON, "LAMENT"

People are interested in birds only inasmuch as they exhibit human behavior—greed and stupidity and anger—and by doing so free us from the unique sorrow of being human.

—DOUGLAS COUPLAND, *LIFE AFTER GOD*, "THINGS THAT FLY"

What Birds Do and How It Applies to Humans (Songs and Singing, Early Birds, Birds as Harbingers, Work, Literature, Birthdays, Sports)

My way is to seize an image that moment it has formed in my mind, to trap it as a bird and to pin it at once to canvas. Afterward I start to tame it, to master it. I bring it under control and I develop it.

—JOAN MIRÓ, LONDON *OBSERVER*

Alight broke in upon my brain,
It was the carol of a bird;
It ceased, and then it came again,
The sweetest song ear ever heard.

—GEORGE GORDON, LORD BYRON, "THE PRISONER OF
CHILLON,"

The smallest birds sing the sweetest; it is always pleasant to hearken to their songs.

—JAMES FENIMORE COOPER, *THE DEERSLAYER*

Down in the forest something stirred:
It was only the note of a bird.

—HAROLD SIMPSON, "DOWN IN THE FOREST"

And yesterday the bird of night did sit,
Even at noon-day, upon the market-place,
Hooting and shrieking.

—WILLIAM SHAKESPEARE, *JULIUS CAESAR*

I see my way as birds their trackless way.
I shall arrive,—what time, what circuit first,
I ask not; but unless God send his hail
Or blinding fire-balls, sleet or stifling snow,
In some time, his good time, I shall arrive:
He guides me and the bird. In his good time.

—ROBERT BROWNING, "PARACELSUS"

A bird arranges
two notes at right angles.

—ELIZABETH BISHOP, "SUNDAY, 4 A.M.," *QUESTIONS OF TRAVEL*

It is a flaw
In happiness to see beyond our bourn,—
It forces us in summer skies to mourn,
It spoils the singing of the Nightingale.

— JOHN KEATS, "EPISTLE TO JOHN HAMILTON REYNOLDS"

Novelists do not write as birds sing, by the push of nature. It is part of the job that there should be much routine and some daily stuff on the level of carpentry.

—WILLIAM GOLDING, "ROUGH MAGIC," LECTURE

Me too the Muses made write verse. I have songs of my own, the shepherds call me also a poet; but I'm not inclined to trust them. For I don't seem yet to write things as good either as Varius or as Cinna, but to be a goose honking among tuneful swans.

—VIRGIL, *ECLOGUES*

The Attic warbler pours her throat,
Responsive to the cuckoo's note.

—THOMAS GRAY, "ODE ON THE SPRING"

List to that bird! His song—what poet pens it?
Brigand of birds, he's stolen every note!
Prince though of thieves—hark! how the rascal
   spends it!
Pours the whole forest from one tiny throat!

—EDNAH PROCTOR HAYES, "THE MOCKING-BIRD"

O Love! has she done this to thee?
What shall, alas! become of me?
What bird so sings, yet so does wail?
O' tis the ravish'd nightingale
Jug, jug, jug, jug, tereu, she cries,
And still her woes at midnight rise.

—JOHN LYLY, "CAMPASPE"

Sometimes a-dropping from the sky
I heard the skylark sing;
Sometimes all little birds that are,
How they seemed to fill the sea and air
With their sweet jargoning!

—SAMUEL TAYLOR COLERIDGE, "RIME OF THE ANCIENT
MARINER"

And hear the pleasant cuckoo, loud and long—
The simple bird that thinks two notes a song.

—W. H. DAVIES, "APRIL'S CHARMS"

Grass grows, birds fly, waves pound the sand. I beat
people up.

—MUHAMMAD ALI, *TIME* MAGAZINE

A poet is a bird of unearthly excellence, who es-
capes from his celestial realm arrives in this world
warbling. If we do not cherish him, he spreads his
wings and flies back into his homeland.

—KAHLIL GIBRAN

Trying to get a fast ball past Hank Aaron is like trying to get the sun past a rooster.

—CURT SIMMONS

Ｉ am a gentleman, though spoiled i' the breeding. The Buzzards are all gentlemen. We came in with the Conqueror.

—RICHARD BROME, *ENGLISH MOOR*

Weighing the stedfastness and state
Of some mean things which here below reside,
Where birds are like watchful Clocks the noiseless
  dat
And Intercourse of times divide,
Where Bees at night get home and hive, and flowrs
Early, aswel as late,
Rise with the Sun, and set in the same bowrs.

—HENRY VAUGHAN, FROM "MAN"

It is remarkable that only small birds properly sing.

—CHARLES DARWIN, THE DESCENT OF MAN

At once a voice arose among
The bleak twigs overhead
In a full-hearted evensong
Of joy unlimited;
An aged thrush, frail, gaunt, and small,
In blast-beruffled plume,
Had chosen thus to fling his soul
Upon the growing gloom.

—THOMAS HARDY, (TWO TITLES) "BY THE CENTURY'S
DEATHBED" AND "THE DARKLING THRUSH"

Everyone suddenly burst out singing;
And I was filled with such delight
As prisoned birds must find in freedom
Winging wildly across the white
Orchards and dark green fields; on; on
and out of sight.
Everyone's voice was suddenly lifted,
And beauty came like the setting sun.
My heart was shaken with tears and horror
Drifted away . . . O but every one
Was a bird; and the song was wordless;
The singing will never be done.

—SIEGFRIED SASSOON, "EVERYONE SANG"

Pisthetaerus: Welcome, Cinesias, you lime-wood man! Why have you come here twisting your game leg in circles?

Cinesias (singing): "I want to become a bird, a tuneful nightingale."

Pisthetaerus: Enough of that sort of ditty. Tell me what you want.

Cinesias: Give me wings and I will fly into the topmost air to gather fresh songs in the clouds, in the midst of the vapors and the fleecy snow.

Pisthetaerus: Gather songs in the clouds?

Cinesias: 'Tis on them the whole of our latter-day art depends. The most brilliant dithyrambs are those that flap their wings in empty space and are clothed

in mist and dense obscurity. To appreciate this, just
listen.

—ARISTOPHANES, "THE BIRDS"

O Blithe New-comer! I have heard,
I hear thee and rejoice.
O Cuckoo! shall I call thee Bird,
Or but a wandering Voice?

Thrice welcome, darling of the Spring!

O blessed Bird! the earth we pace
Again appears to be
An unsubstantial, faery place;
That is fit home for thee!

—WILLIAM WORDSWORTH, "TO THE CUCKOO"

Sweet was the hour, when Nature gave
Her loveliest treasures birth,
And sent these artless choristers
To bless the smiling earth.

—CYNTHIA TAGGART, "THE HAPPY BIRDS," POEMS

Under the greenwood tree
Who loves to lie with me,
And turn his merry note
Unto the sweet bird's throat,
Come hither, come hither, come hither.
Here shall he see
No enemy
But winter and rough weather.

—WILLIAM SHAKESPEARE, AS YOU LIKE IT

I fill this cup to one made up
Of loveliness alone,
A woman, of her gentle sex
The seeming paragon;
To whom the better elements
And kindly stars have given
A form so fair, that, like the air,
'Tis less of earth than heaven.

Her every tone is music's own,
Like those of morning birds,
And something more than melody
Dwells ever in her words;
The coinage of her heart are they,
And from her lips each flows
As one may see the burdened bee
Forth issue from the rose.

—EDWARD C. PINKNEY, "HEALTH"

Come on! Brush your teeth and let's go!
It's your Day of all Days! It's the Best of the Best!
So don't waste a minute!
Hop to it!
Get dressed!

   —DR. SEUSS'S "THE BIRTHDAY BIRD"

Sweet bird, that shunn'st the noise of folly,
Most musical, most melancholy!

—JOHN MILTON, "IL PENSEROSO"

———◆•••◆———

Sweet poet of the woods.

—CHARLOTTE SMITH, "ON THE DEPARTURE OF THE
NIGHTINGALE"

Then he felt quite ashamed, and hid his head under his wings, for he did not know what to do; he was so happy, and yet not at all proud. He thought how he had been persecuted and despised; and now he heard them saying that he was the most beautiful of all birds. Even the elder-tree bent its branches straight down into the water before him, and the sun shone warm and mild. Then his wings rustled, he lifted his slender neck, and cried rejoicingly from the depths of his heart,—

"I never dreamed of so much happiness when I was the Ugly Duckling!"

—HANS CHRISTIAN ANDERSEN, "THE UGLY DUCKLING"

Ye living lamps, by whose dear light
The nightingale does sit so late,
And studying all the summer night,
Her matchless songs does meditate. Ye country
    comets, that portend
No war, nor prince's funeral,
Shining unto no higher end
Then to presage the grasses fall.

—ANDREW MARVELL, "THE MOWER TO THE GLOW-WORMS"

the

hy the caged bird sings,
hen his wing is bruised and his bosom
s his bars and he would be free;
of joy or glee,
he sends from his heart's deep core,
ward to Heaven he flings—
d bird sings!

DUNBAR, THE COMPLETE POEMS,

A Peacock once placed a petition before Juno d[esir]
ing to have the voice of a nightingale in addit[ion to]
his other attractions; but Juno refused his re[quest.]
When he persisted, and pointed out that he [was her]
favourite bird, she said: "Be content with y[our lot;]
one cannot be first in everything."

—AESOP, "THE PEACOCK AND JUNO"

The time of the singing of the birds is come, and [the]
voice of the turtle [dove] is heard in our land.

—THE SONG OF SOLOMON 2:12

Place me on Sunium's marbled steep,
Where nothing, save the waves and I,
May hear our mutual murmurs sweep;
There, swan-like, let me sing and die:
A land of slaves shall ne'er be mine
Dash down yon cup of Samian wine!

—LORD BYRON, "DON JUAN"

O, to be in England
Now that April's there,
And whoever wakes in England
Sees, some morning, unaware,
That the lowest boughs and the brushwood sheaf
Round the elm-tree bole are in tiny leaf,
While the chaffinch sings on the orchard bough
In England—now!

And after April, when May follows,
And the whitethroat builds, and all the swallows!
Hark, where my blossom'd pear-tree in the hedge
Leans to the field and scatters on the clover
Blossoms and dewdrops—at the bent spray's edge—

That's the wise thrush; he sings each song twice
     over,
Lest you should think he never could recapture
The first fine careless rapture!

And though the fields look rough with hoary dew,
All will be gay when noontide wakes anew
The buttercups, the little children's dower
Far brighter than this gaudy melon-flower!

—ROBERT BROWNING, "HOME-THOUGHTS, FROM ABROAD"

The lark now leaves his watery nest
And climbing, shakes his dewy wings;
He takes this window for the east;
And to implore your light, he sings,
Awake, awake, the morn will never rise,
Till she can dress her beauty at your eyes.

—Sir William Davenant, "Song"

Sing on, sweet thrush, upon the leafless bough,
Sing on, sweet bird, I listen to thy strain,
See aged Winter, 'mid his surly reign,
At thy blythe carol, clears his furrowed brow.

—Robert Burns, "Sonnet Written on the Author's Birthday, on hearing a Thrush Sing in His Morning Walk."

Ye living lamps, by whose dear light
The nightingale does sit so late,
And studying all the summer night,
Her matchless songs does meditate. Ye country
    comets, that portend
No war, nor prince's funeral,
Shining unto no higher end
Then to presage the grasses fall.

—ANDREW MARVELL, "THE MOWER TO THE GLOW-WORMS"

A vocabulary that would take the feathers off a hoody crow.

—LILLIAN BECKWITH, *LIGHTLY POACHED*

————•••••————

When amatory poets sing their loves
In liquid lines mellifluously bland,
And pair their rhymes as Venus yokes her doves.

—LORD BYRON, *DON JUAN*

I value my garden more for being full of blackbirds than of cherries, and very frankly give them their fruit for their songs.

—JOSEPH ADDISON

Herald: . . . The bird-madness is so popular that many actually take the names of birds. There is a lame victualler who calls himself Partridge; Menippus calls himself the swallow, Opuntius, the one-eyed crow; Philocles, the lark; Theogenes, the fox-goose; Lycurgus, the ibis; Chaerephon, the bat; Syracusius, the magpie; Midias, the quail: indeed he looks like a quail that has been hit hard on the head. Out of love for the *Birds* they repeat all the songs which concern the swallow, the teal, the goose or the pigeon; in each verse you see wings, or at all events a few feathers. This is what is happening down there. Finally, there are more than ten thousand people who are coming here from earth to ask you for feathers and hooked claws; so mind you supply yourself with wings for the immigrants.

—ARISTOPHANES, "THE BIRDS"

Where the nightingale doth sing
Not a senseless, tranced thing,
But divine melodious truth.

—JOHN KEATS, "BARDS OF PASSION AND OF MIRTH"

———

Birds can be taught various tunes, and even the un-
melodious sparrow has learned to sing like a linnet.

—CHARLES DARWIN, THE DESCENT OF MAN

O Nightingale that on yon blooming spray
Warblest at eve, when all the woods are still,
Thou with fresh hopes the Lover's heart dost fill,
While the jolly Hours lead on propitious May.
Thy liquid notes that close the eye of Day,
First heard before the shallow cuckoo's bill,
Portend success in love. O if Jove's will
Have linked that amorous power to thy soft lay,
Now timely sing, ere the rude bird of hate
Foretell my hopeless doom, in some grove nigh;

As thou from year to year hast sung too late
For my relief, yet had'st no reason why.
Whether the Muse or Love call thee his mate,
Both them I serve, and of their train am I.

—JOHN MILTON, "SONNET TO THE NIGHTINGALE"

Hamlet: But I am pigeon-liver'd, and lack gall
To make oppression bitter, or ere this
I should have fatted all the region kites
With this slave's offal. Bloody, bawdy villain!
Remorseless, treacherous, lecherous, kindless
   villain!

—WILLIAM SHAKESPEARE, *HAMLET*

The moans of doves in immemorial elms,
And murmuring of innumerable bees.

—ALFRED LORD TENNYSON, *THE PRINCESS*, "COME DOWN O
MAID, FROM YONDER MOUNTAIN HEIGHT"

Blackbirds are the cellos of the deep farms.

—ANNE STEVENSON, "GREEN MOUNTAIN, BLACK
MOUNTAIN," *MINUTE BY GLASS MINUTE*

———◆•◆•◆———

Cuckoo-echoing, bell-swarmèd, lark-charmèd,
rook-racked, river-rounded.

—GERARD MANLEY HOPKINS, "DUNS SCOTUS' OXFORD"

At the corner of Wood Street, when daylight
  appears,
Hangs a Thrush that sings loud, it has sung for
  three years:
Poor Susan has pass'd by the spot, and has heard
In the silence of morning the song of the bird.

'Tis a note of enchantment; what ails her? She sees
A mountain ascending, a vision of trees;
Bright volumes of vapour through Lothbury glide,
And a river flows on through the vale of Cheapside.

Green pastures she views in the midst of the dale
Down which she so often has tripp'd with her pail;

And a single small cottage, a nest like a dove's,
The one only dwelling on earth that she loves.

She looks, and her heart is in heaven: but they fade,
The mist and the river, the hill and the shade;
The stream will not flow, and the hill will not rise,
And the colours have all pass'd away from her eyes!

—WILLIAM WORDSWORTH, "THE REVERIE OF POOR SUSAN"

O Nightingale! thou surely art
A creature of a "fiery heart":
These notes of thine—they pierce and pierce;
Tumultuous harmony and fierce!

—WILLIAM WORDSWORTH, "O NIGHTINGALE"

Portia: The crow doth sing as sweetly as the lark
When neither is attended, and I think
The nightingale, if she should sing by day,
When every goose is cackling, would be though'
No better a musician than the wren.

—WILLIAM SHAKESPEARE, *THE MERCHANT OF VENICE*

"I dare say you're wondering why I don't put my arm round your waist," said the Duchess, after a pause: "the reason is, that I'm doubtful about the temper of your flamingo. Shall I try the experiment?"

"He might bite," Alice cautiously replied, not feeling at all anxious to have the experiment tried.

"Very true," said the Duchess: "flamingoes and mustard both bite. And the moral of that is—'Birds of a feather flock together.'"

"Only mustard isn't a bird," Alice remarked.

"Right, as usual," said the Duchess. "What a clear way you have of putting things!"

—LEWIS CARROLL, *ALICE IN WONDERLAND*

Some social birds apparently call to each other for aid; and as they flit from tree to tree the flock is kept together by chirp answering chirp.

—CHARLES DARWIN, *THE DESCENT OF MAN*

Under the greenwood tree
Who loves to lie with me,
And turn his merry note
Unto the sweet bird's throat,
Come hither, come hither, come hither.

—WILLIAM SHAKESPEARE, *As You Like It*

Edward: His name that valiant duke hath left with
  thee;
His dukedom and his chair with me is left.

Richard: Nay, if thou be that princely eagle's bird,
Show thy descent by gazing 'gainst the sun:
For chair and dukedom, throne and kingdom say;
Either that is thine, or else thou wert not his.

—WILLIAM SHAKESPEARE, *King Henry the Sixth*

At the close of the day when the hamlet is still,
And mortals the sweets of forgetfulness prove,
When naught but the torrent is heard on the hill,
And naught but the nightingale's song in the grove.

—JAMES BEATTIE, "THE HERMIT"

———◦•••◦———

What time's the next swan?

—LEO SLEZAK WHEN A MECHANICAL SWAN EXITED THE STAGE
WITHOUT HIM DURING A PERFORMANCE OF *LOHENGRIN*

Juliet: 'Tis almost morning; I would have thee gone;
And yet no further than a wanton's bird,
Who lets it hop a little from her hand,
Like a poor prisoner in his twisted gyves,
And with a silk thread plucks it back again,
So loving-jealous of his liberty.

Romeo: I would I were thy bird.

Juliet: Sweet, so would I:
Yet I should kill thee with much cherishing.
Good night, good night! parting is such sweet
  sorrow
That I shall say good night till it be morrow.
—WILLIAM SHAKESPEARE, *ROMEO AND JULIET*

The host with someone indistinct
Converses at the door apart,
The nightingales are singing near
The Convent of the Sacred Heart.

—T. S. ELIOT, *POEMS*, "SWEENEY AMONG THE
NIGHTINGALES"

Her prose is like a bird darting from place to place, palpitating with nervous energy; but a bird with a bright beady eye and a sharp beak as well.

—FRANCIS HOPE ON MURIEL SPARK

Ah, what can ail thee, wretched wight,
Alone and palely loitering;
The sedge is wither'd from the lake,
And no birds sing.

—JOHN KEATS, "ISABELLA"

Minnie or Susy or Mae, middle-aging behind the counter, hair curled and rouge and powder on a sweating face. Taking orders in a soft low voice, calling them to the cook with a screech like a peacock.

—JOHN STEINBECK, *THE GRAPES OF WRATH*

Come, fill the Cup, and in the Fire of Spring
Your Winter Garment of Repentance fling:
The Bird of Time has but a little way
To fly—and Lo! the Bird is on the Wing.

—EDWARD FITZGERALD, "RUBAIYAT OF OMAR KHAYYAM"

The sound of the harpsichord resembles that of a bird-cage played with toasting-forks.

—THOMAS BEECHAM, BRITISH CONDUCTOR

Poetry is a rich, full-bodied whistle, cracked ice crunching in pails, the night that numbs the leaf, the duel of two nightingales, the sweet pea that has run wild, Creation's tears in shoulder blades.

—BORIS PASTERNAK, *LIFE* MAGAZINE

A widow bird sate mourning for her Love
Upon a wintry bough;
The frozen wind crept on above
The freezing stream below.

There was no leaf upon the forest bare,
No flower upon the ground,
And little motion in the air
Except the mill-wheel's sound.

—PERCY BYSSHE SHELLEY, "A WIDOW BIRD"

. . . During the next twenty-four hours I saw and heard, either right around the house or while walking down to bathe, through the woods, the following forty-two birds:

Little green heron, night heron, red-tailed hawk, yellow-billed cuckoo, kingfisher, flicker, hummingbird, swift, meadow-lark, red-winged blackbird, sharp-tailed finch, song sparrow, chipping sparrow, bush sparrow, purple finch, Baltimore oriole, cowbunting, robin, wood thrush, thrasher, catbird, scarlet tanager, red-eyed vireo, yellow warbler, black-throated green warbler, kingbird, wood peewee, crow, blue jay, cedar-bird, Maryland yellowthroat, chickadee, black and white creeper, barn swallow, white-breasted swallow, ovenbird, thistlefinch, vesperfinch, indigo bunting, towhee, grasshopper-sparrow, and screech owl.

The birds were still in song, for on Long Island there is little abatement in the chorus until about the second week of July, when the blossoming of the chestnut trees patches the woodland with frothy greenish-yellow.

—THEODORE ROOSEVELT, "OUTDOORS AND INDOORS," *THEODORE ROOSEVELT: AN AUTOBIOGRAPHY*

About the Author

Bill Adler Jr. is the author of numerous books about birds and birdwatching. He lives in Washington, D.C., with his wife P. Robin (a kind of bird) and two daughters. Adler's Web site is www.adlerbooks.com.

Index